# SUCCESSFUL FIELD SERVICE MANAGEMENT

# SUCCESSFUL
# FIELD SERVICE
# MANAGEMENT

## Donald N. McCafferty

A DIVISION OF AMERICAN MANAGEMENT ASSOCIATIONS

Library of Congress Cataloging in Publication Data

McCafferty, Donald N
  Successful field service management.

  Includes index.
  1.  Service industries—Management.  I.  Title.
HD9980.5.M32      338.4'7      79-54842
ISBN 0-8144-5583-2

First Printing

# Preface

This is a book about creating a service business and managing it for those first tender years when most of the critical decisions are made. It is based on my personal experiences in service and service-related businesses over a period of almost 30 years. During that period I have made at least once most of the mistakes that could be made. In some of those cases, the people who knew how to do it right had not passed that information along to me. They probably assumed that either I already had the information or could develop it myself so easily that I needed no help. There are multitudes of ways to accomplish things that "just aren't talked about." The old-timers know, but it's not something they normally discuss, and for the same reason—it is something everyone is already supposed to know.

I have tried to bring that kind of information into the open. This is a "how-to' book—how to establish a service department and how to run a service department. It is *not* a book on management theory. After defining the objectives, this book will show you how to accomplish what must be done. In some instances I will point out things that perhaps you would not ordinarily have seen the need for but that are in reality quite necessary—things that we have all left out of our planning at times, which were the eventual cause of either reduced success or complete failure of a project.

There is another rather compelling reason for writing a book. Deep in the heart of each of us there is an urge to become a prophet—a person with a message—and we would all like to preach the gospel we believe in. I will, therefore, inject my personal philosophy on how best to run a business. I believe that, properly created and organized, a service business can perform a worthwhile service and make a good profit at the same time.

No one does a thing like this alone, and I have had a lot of help: My wife, Kathleen, who spent a long time watching me wrestle with a typewriter and listening to me mumble to myself. My boss for many years, Joe Bowers, one of the best businessmen I know. Another former boss, Don Schmidt, who at one time forced me to stop running a business by the old maxim, "When in trouble, when in doubt, run in circles, scream and shout." A guy named Tom Burns who, while working for me, used to make me explain why I was doing something a particular way, why I was taking so long to do it, and why I was not doing it his way. A fellow named Dale Bellows, who developed a technique for keeping me humble. Some others who, whether they knew it or not, contributed heavily to the ideas behind the writing of this book: Al Lucas, Ed Dill, Cliff Martin, Steve Fabian, Tim Burns, Ross Nelson, Bob Page, and Wayne McCarthy. And during the years I have been in management, there have been all those unsung heroes who, while I was telling them how to do something, were teaching me that there just might be a better way.

DONALD N. McCAFFERTY

# Special credit

*Special credit is given to the National Association of Service Managers for permission to use material from its Service Executive's Digest entitled "Training Field Managers," which I wrote for them in 1976.*

*NASM is a national association of product service executives. The objectives of NASM are to provide service management education and to promote the status of service executives in the business community. It provides a variety of publications, seminars, conferences, and institutes, including a series of service management executive development programs at major universities. It also provides a forum for the exchange of technological and managerial information among service managers.*

# Contents

# 1

# Setting up a service ~~department~~ business

THE OBJECTIVE of this book is to help determine the best way for you to create and manage a service business effectively—more specifically, how to establish the business, how to determine and implement the initial policies that will help to form its personality, and how to nurse it through those first, formative years.

A business does have a personality of its own. It is aggressive or shy, boisterous or restrained, progressive or cautious. I submit that the business personality is imprinted by you, its creator. Through many years of managers who succeed you, the personality may slowly and gradually change, but you and your ideas will be recognizable for a long time. You will always be the father of the child. Jobs will exist that didn't exist before, corporate images will be formed, families will be started because someone now has a job, and careers will begin.

People spend about 12 hours a day either working or traveling to and from work—half their lives! The atmosphere and the environment of their workplace will have more impact on their life-style than most other things. Creating something that will be of such primary importance to so many people is an awesome responsibility. It is therefore important for us as the creators to understand the far-reaching effects of our actions, and to ensure that the expected effects have some impact on how we begin.

What is your reason for starting a new business? Are you starting from scratch? Reorganizing? Expanding? Whichever is true for you, this book will help you collect and organize your ideas so you can perform effectively. Effective, by the way, means "producing the intended or expected result." Throughout this book the term "effective" will be used in place of "efficient," which merely means having and using the requisite skill, knowledge, and industry, but makes no mention of results.

Changes in the marketplace in this decade have moved the service business into the inner circle of top management. This change in the status of service as a business appears to have several causes. Consumerism and the activities of consumer advocate organizations have caused changes in public attitudes that have made the consumer environment much more demanding. Legislation affecting both the consumer and the commercial–industrial marketplace is regulating more and more of the manufacturer–customer relationship after the sale of the product. Related to this is the doctrine of strict liability developed in our courts, under which a manufacturer may be held liable for damage or injury resutling from the use of its products even if the product is not defective and negligence is not involved. Another factor is the increasingly complex technology of today's products. The customer necessarily has to depend more on the manufacturer's ability to provide a service organization that can keep his products operable.

Service is the primary interface with customers after the product is sold. It is no longer an unpleasant duty. Rather, it is an essential feature of the product. It has also begun to have a much greater impact on other management functions. It can affect procedures in every department of the company. Accordingly, communication has improved between service and the sales, marketing, legal, engineering, and manufacturing departments.

Since service is the major source of information on how products operate in the field, many, if not most, product improvements are a result of service feedback. Service is the function that spots product hazards as they occur, and can alert the customer to the hazard and the company to the liability exposure. It is the essential component of the management team that is responsible for the decision to stop production or shipment of a hazardous or malfunctioning component. By fixing the responsibility for the defect, failure, or hazard, it can determine which part of the organization should bear the cost of making good.

There is a noticeable trend in industry as a whole toward making service executives responsible for managing profit centers. This pursuit of profit, along with the furnishing of funds to the parent company, has helped service do a better job, since the manager is in the position of an entrepreneur who is forced by the pressures of competition to make a profit while providing a marketable service at a price acceptable to the customer.

At this point, let's assume that—for whatever reason—you are going to establish a service business within your company, a large national corporation. (These ideas will work just as well for an individual starting a business.) You have a choice: you can let the business grow by itself, as many of us have done, and learn the lessons the hard way, or you can make the basic directional decisions at the start.

I used a little trick in the chapter title, crossing out the word "department" and substituting the word "business." Obviously, I was trying to make a point. You may call service a department because it is a part of some other organizational unit, but it *is* a business —it has to be conceptualized as a business and, once started, it has to be run like a business.

One of the first things to be settled is why you want to start a service business in the first place. What we're after is not the stated reason, but the *real* reason. The answer to this question is necessary so you can decide what kind of a service business to design. Here are a few possibilities:

- *Your boss told you to.* If this is all you've got worked out so far, you had better get back to the drawing board.
- *Customers have been complaining.* Now there's a good reason! What they may be saying is that after they buy one of your products, they don't know where to turn when it stops working.
- *You want to make money.* Although you may not think so right now, this is a very logical and practical reason.
- *You want to improve the company image.* At first glance this may seem like an excellent reason, but I'll bet there is more behind it.
- *You need to comply with consumer laws.* This is a legitimate reason, but there are bound to be others in the background.

You are in the process of designing a business. You must decide what kind of business it will be, and set the basic goals and objectives of the business. To do this properly, you need to know why you are starting this business. The odds are that uncovering the real reasons will take some effort. You will have to ask a lot of questions and pin people down—but you have to know. If the original decision comes from an executive vice-president three management levels above your boss, you may have to get an appointment and ask him. This is preferable to the frustration of setting the business up, running it for a year, and then getting the word to shut it down because it was not doing what the big man had expected it to.

The reason the initial decisions are so important is that even if some specifics will not be implemented for years, the form and direction of the business will have been preordained. Let's define these basic decisions.

## COST OR PROFIT CENTER

Whether you are starting a cost or a profit center is perhaps the most important choice of all. Historically, most service operations that are a part of a larger company started as cost centers. The company saw the need for a department to provide certain services to customers, and set up a "service department." This department usually reported to the sales or marketing group, and was regarded as one of the evils necessary to answer the complaints of customers. A budget was established, and the department's job became to perform whatever tasks were assigned by the sales group —without exceeding the cost plan. Not only was there no desire to make a profit, but the very idea of doing so was regarded as a disservice to the customer and sometimes even as disloyalty to the company and its goals. We will discuss these ideas in more detail later in the chapter.

The best time to decide whether the new business should be a cost or a profit center is at the beginning. Even when there is agreement that it is to be a cost center, the subject should be discussed, and discussed seriously. Perhaps you should stress the point that if the future holds even the remote possibility of profitability, it should be part of the initial planning.

If the business is to start as a cost center and within a specific number of years shift to a profit orientation, the desired result must be incorporated into the initial organization and running of the business. The expectation of a profit, even some time in the future, tends to sharpen the operation. The staff looks for effective cost control rather than merely worrying about not going over budget.

Again, let me emphasize that even though the best option for your company may be a cost center, the question of profit now or later should be discussed thoroughly so that all concerned will have no doubt about what the real long-range goals are.

### Cost center

Depending on the functions the service operation is to perform and how they are to be financed by the company, there are some choices as to how to set up the cost center. One way is to calculate the cost of manpower and facilities to perform the assigned tasks and set up a budget to cover those costs. Another method, the favorite of some computer companies, is to calculate the cost of service performance and develop it as a percentage of sales. From that point on, that percentage of sales becomes the service budget. Each time another sale is made, your budget goes up and you will have work to do.

The basic problem with the cost center is that it becomes like the government in that you are expected to spend your entire budget but not go over it—and everyone knows that if you do not use it all, you will not get as much next year! No matter how you may protest that you won't operate that way, you will. It may be the only way to run a government (this could be the basis for several books and a few elections) but it is a hell of a way to run a business.

### Profit center

If you are to be a profit center, there are all sorts of operating techniques to establish and decisions to make, and that is really what this book is all about. We will get to the details in later chapters. However, some basic philosophies of business operation must be discussed. First of all, what profit level do you wish to maintain? Believe it or not, that is a decision you make consciously, not something that happens to you as time goes on. So first you must agree with your management on the desired profit level. It can really be whatever you want. You decide what it must be, and then take whatever steps are required to meet that goal.

Stated in an admittedly oversimplified way, you first decide what functions you will perform, figure out what it would cost to perform them, and then establish your pricing to deliver the required level of profit. Then you have to determine whether your services are good enough to command these prices from the customers. If you have a marketable service, it really is that simple. What other things do you have to do?

Performance *must* be maintained if you are to be anything other than the lowest priced company in your industry. Controls must be established from the beginning. There needs to be rigid control of the pricing structure, of the costs, and of operating procedures.

Throughout your organization, there must be a very clear understanding that you are established as a profit center, and that you will not be giving away your product (service) at the request of other departments (probably sales or marketing).

## DEFINING YOUR REAL OBJECTIVES

The next challenge is the definition of the real objectives compared with the imagined ones. Here is an example. The company has been taking care of customer complaints for years by passing them off on dealers, but this will not work any more, so it has decided to organize a service department. You have been in quality control and have some sales experience, so you are tapped for the job. Naturally, top management has discussed it, and the following instructions are passed along to you:

> Go ahead and organize a service department. You can pull the necessary people from several other departments, including the secretarial pool. Talk to your new boss, the sales manager, about a budget. Advertising will help you get a few mailings out to the dealers. This should not really be a big deal; just keep the customers from sending any more letters to Washington.

Many people who are now successful service managers will tell you they started their organizations just about that way. You cannot really fault the company for such a cavalier approach. The people who run the company usually have either sales or finance backgrounds, and the odds are that they have never even been in the service business. Their approach is the same as it would be to something they have done a thousand times before—just go and do it! After all, *everybody* knows how to do *that!*

So here you are with the fuzziest objectives anyone has ever had. You have to walk the fine line between forcing your superiors to answer so many questions that they decide you are not the one for a new venture and trying to do the job with so little real direction you do not know which way to turn. How far you can go in getting back to the big boss depends on the size and setup of your company. In most cases you may have to settle for your immediate boss.

The first thing you have to face is that it is up to you and you alone. You have to define the real objectives, set realistic goals, make the basic decisions—and then sell what you have done, and plan to do, to management. If you have sales experience in your background it will surely help, for you are about to embark on the greatest and most exciting sales campaign of your life —the creation of a business!

Let's spend some time on the real versus the imagined objectives, since they will be the basis of your working out what has to be done. In the examples to follow, I will call them "stated" and "real." Read carefully. If you do not pay attention, you may make the assumption that what is said is what your superiors really mean.

| *Stated Objective* | *Real Objective* |
|---|---|
| Go ahead and organize a service department. | Develop a plan for the organization of a service department. |
| Pull people from other departments. | Develop a plan for the organization of a service department. |
| Talk to your boss about the budget. | After you have done all the rest, work out a *complete* cost plan. |
| Get a few mailings out to the dealers. | Decide who will provide the service—dealers, wholesalers, or factory. |
| Keep the customers from writing those letters. | Decide what services are necessary for customer satisfaction and how to supply them. |
| (No objective stated) | Decide if it should be a profit or a cost center. |
| (No objective stated) | Decide how much time you need. |
| (No objective stated) | Decide what products should be serviced. |

Accomplishing these objectives is your problem, and you spend the first days or weeks planning and thinking instead of running around in circles putting the wrong wheels in motion. The objectives we have been discussing can also be sorted into short- and long-range objectives. Although you may wish to be a profit center, good sense could dictate starting as a cost center for a few years while you learn the business, or while you sort out what your customers want and will buy. This approach also gives you an opportunity to organize your business, to get the kinks out and the people trained while the company is supporting your endeavors without putting you under immediate pressure to produce a profit. It might be well to phase in all the other objectives also.

If you can get the assistance of your company comptroller, consider making a long-term cost and profit analysis. These days they are called financial models and are done on a computer. Without going into too much detail, it is a matter of putting all the parts of your business together with the costs associated with them, and calculating what will happen over a period of five or ten years.

Done properly, a cost and profit analysis will show you in which year you will turn the corner and go in the black and exactly how much it will cost the company for you to get there. It will also give you a chance to play "what if" games and get a feel for what you can do to change the timing. You will be better able to judge the effects of various actions.

When it is all put together, polished, and refined, such an analysis is a beautiful thing indeed to present to top management. It can be done effectively by hand with a calculator, but it takes longer and it is more difficult to handle several variables at one time with a calculator. But if computer time is not available to you, be assured that cost and profit analyses can be and have been done by hand.

At some point along the way the goals have to become realistic. It is natural for management to want a task completed in one year, but in reality it may take two or three. Management may want to turn the corner into profitability in three years, but five may be more realistic. Any task may be accomplished in more or less time than was first imagined. To be done in less time than was originally calculated takes a larger investment in people and money.

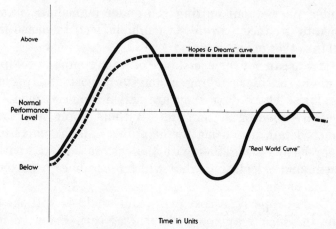

**Figure 1. A typical pattern of business performance: quick accomplishment, precipitate decline, and eventual leveling off.**

Normal, expected, and realistic results are plotted in Figure 1. The horizontal baseline represents normal performance—whatever that happens to be for your activity. The dotted curve represents what management really expects in most cases. The new organization should, within a set time period (let's say a month), go from the zero starting point to something better than normal (which is what management really wanted in the first place) and then stay there for good, only rarely if ever falling back to the normal level.

The solid curve shows what will almost always happen in the real world. From the zero starting point you will zoom to the top of the world in performance within a few months, surpassing even the wildest hopes of management. At about that time Murphy's Law will take over, and all the wrong things that can happen will. After that first month or so, when you surprise everyone with your brilliant management, the things that are wrong will show up and things will go to hell. It will normally only be for a few months, but things will be terrible. Then what is good management on your part, and has been the whole time, will take over—the problems will be solved, the systems will be refined, the people will be trained, the material shortages will go away, your boss will realize that he picked the best person after all, and the curve will cycle above and below the normal performance level.

You must realize that the solid line is the real world of Murphy's Law, and that this is what you and your management should expect and plan for. If you do, it will result in better understanding of what is happening, and a lot less of your time will have to be spent explaining to everyone who will listen just how this curve works. The real challenge is in defining objectives, establishing realistic goals, and reaching agreement with management on how the goals are to be implemented.

## DECIDING ON WHAT SERVICE TO PERFORM

There are, as usual, several choices of the kind of service you will perform, and the one you select will be based largely on the activities of your company and the type of product it puts out.

- *Product in warranty.* This requires you to service the products of your company while they are in warranty, and ordinarily you will not be charging for the service.
- *Products of other manufacturers.* Many companies have a hang-up on this subject, having decided that there is something unethical about servicing the products of other manufacturers. It is not only ethical but necessary in what is now a service-oriented world. Although there is usually some similarity in the products serviced (type of product, used together in a common environment), this is not a re-

quirement. For example, a typewriter manufacturer might well consider servicing typewriters manufactured by others; or a company manufacturing and servicing industrial electronics on earth-moving and paving machinery might provide service on the hydraulic systems associated with their equipment. Another example would be a manufacturer of refrigeration compressors extending its services to include complete heating and air-conditioning systems, controls, air filters, and so on.

□ *Pure service.* This includes the performance and selling of services on products not in allied markets, or services that are not dependent on a particular product. Examples would be janitorial services, building management, and other such services where status as a manufacturer is not pertinent.

## SOME OTHER THINGS TO DECIDE

Are you to be a cost or profit center? What are the real objectives, as defined after lengthy discussion between you and your management? Are there short-range goals that change after the first year? What will be the basic philosophy of the business? The important thing to remember here is the difference between what you imagine your management wants and what it really wants. The only way to settle this is for you to develop your plans along the lines you think most realistic and then work out an agreement with management.

What is the time frame of the objectives assigned you? Are the objectives realistic? Are they based on desire or reality? What are the boundaries, the amounts, or the numbers? How many things must be serviced? How many people will it take to do it? What costs are involved? What are the budgeting procedures? What planning is required? When must it be complete?

There is another matter of prime importance that

must be mentioned. Most companies these days operate on management by objectives (MBO), at least to some degree, and as a result you will at some point be assigned some personal objectives. Since your personal promotional and financial future will depend on your performance against objectives, you must do your best to keep from being locked into first-year objectives that are actually based on how your new organization should be operating after several years of hard work and effort. As your objectives are written, and you agree to them, be sure that they are realistic and attainable. If they are not, it could have a negative effect on your future. So these are the questions and problems that must somehow be solved by you, the new expert. Although you may never have done anything like this before, you have to solve them. And although your corporate experience prior to this may have involved moving into positions vacated by other people, you are now the one to engineer the creation of a business. So if we assume that you have done your homework and developed the necessary plans, forecasts, and predictions, and that you have answered the important questions for yourself, now comes the supreme challenge: it's time to sell the entire concept to management.

## SELLING THE CONCEPT TO MANAGEMENT

In the beginning, management decided there was to be a service department within the company, and you were selected to head it up. You were given general guidelines and a general direction. From that time on it has been your responsibility to put the whole program together and get it ready. In other words, your responsibility has been to take the initial steps in creating the new business. Now that you have done this, you have a new responsibility: presenting the entire concept to management people in such a way that they will understand what you intend to do, how you intend to do it, what it will cost, and what the results will be—and then approve your plan.

Remember that you are trying to sell the idea of establishing a business that has not previously existed in your company, a business that operates on concepts to which most of traditional management is unaccustomed. This is the kind of business that, when it operates in a manner that will allow it to succeed, will violate many of the tried and true principles of business which people in top management cherish. However, it is the kind of business that will, if operated effectively, be profitable far beyond their expectations, and that can pay back their investment many times over—but it must be run differently than the "regular" business they are used to.

## Overcoming some of management's specific objections

There will, of course, be technical objections—the investment required, the effort needed to initiate the business, and so on. Since these are based on specifics, they can generally be answered by specifics. The objections difficult to answer, however, will be those based on the differences between the service business and the business with which most management people are familiar. To you, or to another experienced service executive, these objections may be groundless, but to higher-echelon executives, they can be formidable.

One of the first objections will probably be what we might call the "sales tool syndrome." In the experience of the company to date, when service was performed at all, it was given to the customer as a sales incentive. If a large enough customer has a problem, and you solve the problem for him, the odds are good that he will buy your product again. You cannot react to this one by calling it ridiculous, because it isn't. It's true that when you satisfy the needs of a customer he will return for more of the same. Here are some other considerations.

□ A service function, like any other function, is performed more effectively when people have a logical and motivating reason for doing so. When a product is to be fixed only because a customer has demanded it, the people responsible will exert only the amount of effort necessary to solve the specific complaint—and that's all. When these functions are performed by the members of a group who exist specifically to perform service in a professional manner, and are proud of their capability to do so, it will be done in a professional manner.

□ Your company has profit goals, as do all companies. The performance of services on a nonpaying basis during a warranty period can be considered quite a normal procedure, and the cost of such services is without doubt included in the original selling price. When the performance of such services extends over a longer time period than the one covered by the warranty, and the costs are not recovered in the sales price, it eats into the profits very rapidly. All businessmen, including your customers, understand this basic fact of life, and do not really expect free services forever.

As a group, salespeople have a tendency to say things like, "It won't ever need any repairs, but if it should, just call us and we will take care of it." As we have said, customers as a whole understand that there is no such thing as a free lunch. This may require some retraining of salespeople so that they won't make statements like that. If you have had experience in the service business, you may recognize this as somewhat of an understatement.

◻ Any good businessman will understand what you mean when you explain that although you provide certain services during the warranty period, he also has certain responsibilities. Exactly what these are will, of course, depend on your product, your corporate policy, and the practices of your industry. He will also understand what you are saying when you explain that during the warranty period you will (for a price) shoulder those responsibilities for him, and that after the warranty has expired you will be there to assist him in his hour of need—again, for a price.

Over the years, as your services are performed in a highly professional manner, your salespeople will come to realize that your operational professionalism is by far the best sales tool they have.

Another common objection by management to establishing a service business—and probably one of the more strenuous ones—is the competitive angle. If your product is sold to the ultimate consumer through dealers or contractors who are to any degree at all in the service business, you will be said to be in direct competition with your own best customers. This will immediately become an emotional issue whose first effect may be the destruction of your presentation.

However, this objection can be answered calmly and logically. For one thing, the chances are that you will not be offering the same services, or quality of services, that your customers do—yours may be more general or more specialized. Your services may be priced either above or below the competition's, but they will be different. If you intend to offer a very high quality of services, you will create more business for your customers than they can handle. This will be the result of your locating a service customer and creating in him a need for the services you offer. When he looks for a lower price, your competitors will get a good share of the business. It is also true that in the service business there is enough for everyone. Some time in the distant future the market may become saturated, but in the foreseeable future the business is there for those who will go after it and who do it well.

And again, there is the cost-profit concept. If you have in fact done your homework, you will have a lovely plan all laid out showing the impact on the corporation of developing a service department which, over a period of 4.7 years, will become a profit center rather than a cost center. The odds are that initially people in top management will be thinking of it as a cost center. But if you are able to show them its potential to be a profit center, you will certainly get their undivided attention.

## Speak to management people in their own language

It's most important that you use the language of management in making such a presentation. You must try to anticipate what their questions and objections will be, and not only have responses for them, but if possible answer them even before they have been asked. If they think in terms of ROA (return on assets), use ROA. If it's ROI (return on investment), use that. If it's profit before income tax (PBIT), cost avoidance, or long-term growth, learn to understand and use these terms. If you talk to top-management people in the language of a salesman, a quality control engineer, or an administrator. they will neither understand nor approve of what you say. Basically their language is the language of business and finance, so for a time you must become adept at business and finance.

But while you're trying to sell your plan to management, always keep one thing in mind:

## McCAFFERTY'S LAW NUMBER ONE
### No one understands your business as well as you do. You will spend the rest of your life explaining it to others.

With this perspective. you'll be able to do a better selling job.

## DEVELOP A SENSE OF MISSION—AND STICK TO IT!

Then there is always the magnificent vision. For a man to be a successful businessman, he has to be an entrepreneur, a creator, and a bit of a dreamer. He needs to operate with a sense of mission. When you are starting a completely new organization—even though it may look like a mere flyspeck on the corporate organization chart—it's your business: there are all those frontiers to be explored, wild animals to be tamed, and worlds to be conquered! Don't feel embarrassed because you see these opportunities, and because you dream dreams of what the future can hold. You are perhaps one of the few people in the whole corporation who has researched it completely enough to realize that these are not idle dreams; they are projects to be accomplished. Of course you'll have to convince management and all the people who work for you that you're not some kind of a nut! You can see something they can't see, and when you make it happen, they will begin to believe you.

It is almost impossible to get everyone in any group to be able to see what the future can hold, and to operate with a sense of mission. Any organization that could do this would be able to accomplish anything it wanted to. But there will be a few of you—yourself and a small number of others—who believe, and because they believe, they will accomplish things. Some few others will go to their retirement convinced that you *are* crazy, even when you're successful.

# 2

# Organization: Structural problems and physical needs

A VERY BASIC organizational question to be resolved is whether your new business will be company-owned, or operated through dealer-distributors. This decision is sometimes almost automatic, depending on how your particular industry seems to operate, but it is an important enough decision to merit some thought.

A primary consideration should be how you want it to operate five or more years from now. Should it be your intent to eventually operate as an entirely in-house service group, you must consider the problems to be encountered in making such a basic and earth-shaking change in an organization that was begun in another manner. It will in fact be much easier to effect the change in the other direction (from in-house to dealer) should the need arise.

At first glance this decision may seem to have been foreordained by the type of product you manufacture. The service industry is very flexible, however, and you will find a variety of products handled by dealer-distributor organizations, including small appliances, electronic equipment, cars and trucks, heavy equipment, and power tools. On the other hand, some of the products serviced by in-house company-owned groups are small appliances, electronic equipment, cars and trucks, heavy equipment, and power tools. So it appears that again the choice is yours. Let's look at some of the advantages and disadvantages of company-owned as opposed to in-house businesses.

## A COMPANY-OWNED BUSINESS

*Advantages.* The entire organization will be a part of the company, and you will have control of organization, staffing, procedures, and all the decisions that must be made in a new and expanding organization.

In creating a new business, you will have expenses that may not be recoverable for some time. If you are a part of the company, financing is not a problem. Of course, it must be planned, approved, and controlled, but you will have the resources of the company behind you. You will have operational control in that every time you wish to implement a policy change, be it technical or not, you can do so within your own organization without having to persuade each of the dealers and distributors.

In the area of financing, each of the dealer-distributors will certainly be a profit center. Therefore any business they perform for you must be profitable for them, or they will show a marked lack of desire to perform it at all.

*Disadvantages.* In a completely new organization, you will have to start from the beginning and train each and every person. This can mean a considerable expenditure of money and effort. If you are in fact trailblazing a new business within your company, there will undoubtedly be difficulties in getting all the necessary approvals for procedures and policies, since those who must approve also lack a complete understanding of the special needs of the service business. A corollary to this point is that your policies and procedures will in large part be dictated by those of the parent corporation.

## A DEALER-DISTRIBUTOR ORGANIZATION

The advantages and disadvantages of a dealer-distributor organization are largely the reverse of those noted above, but should be examined in different terms and from a different viewpoint.

*Advantages.* If the dealers and distributors who provide service are chosen carefully, you will start with a force of trained and capable people who are also familiar with your product (and very probably with its service). Under this system, the local businesses are already in operation as profit centers, and the only financing involved will be the cost of their expansion into service. In addition, you need not be concerned with the nitty-gritty details of a service business's day-to-day operation, such as sick time, truck breakdown, and so on, because these are strictly the problems of the dealer.

*Disadvantages.* Every change you wish to make in policies or procedures must be sold to every dealer-distributor, each of whom is an individual businessman who will not blindly accept anything you say but must be convinced it is to his advantage. (I must add at this point that the same problems exist for the company that deals with field offices operating as profit centers, but I'll examine that in more detail later on. Whichever choice you make, there is going to be someone out there keeping you on your toes!)

One fundamental problem you will face with a dealer-distributor organization is that it's just not your company—the loyalties will not be the same, and you have no right to expect them to be. You will also have difficulty in maintaining as much control as you would like to have over such matters as pricing and cost. Negotiations with customers who have problems can sometimes be made more difficult by the additional people in the middle.

## GEOGRAPHY, LINE VS. STAFF ORGANIZATION, AND OTHER MATTERS

But there are other factors to be considered, and decisions must be made about them, too. As was noted earlier, these decisions are better made in the beginning and your direction established for the future, because changes of this type are very difficult to make after a business has already taken shape.

First, there's the matter of geography. Are you going to cover the entire nation at the start? Or perhaps your products are distributed on a local or regional basis, which will make the initial decision simpler. But again, we must plan for the future. If you plan to provide your services on a national basis, your organization must of course be set up that way. We're back again to the matter of starting small and graduating to the larger organization as the business matures. You can very well start an organization by having yourself, a secretary, and three service people located in your home office. Each of the service people can handle a third of the nation while you build the business. Twenty years later you may have several thousand people in your service business. It can happen, and has happened to more companies than you can imagine.

The geographical question is a matter of planning for the future. If you are planning for growth, you should set up your organization in such a manner that someday having to appoint regional managers and perhaps regional staffs will not tear the organization apart. If it can be set up in such a way that it will not have to be done over and over again as the business grows, so much the better. When there is a complete shuffle every few years, people start measuring their time until retirement on the basis of surviving just one more reorganization.

The use of line and staff organizations is practically a science, and literature on the subject is abundant, so I will not dwell on the details. However, a few points of major importance must be considered. One is control, both the source and the proper amount. As to the source, you must consider from what position you wish to maintain control, and of what material. Some things are better controlled locally; some cannot be. The amount of control depends on the matter to be controlled, and whether it is best to control it rigidly or loosely. It's usually best to control loosely and leave room for individuality, but where you need a very specific result, control!

To really accomplish the assigned goals, an organization must be both flexible and effective. As your organization grows, your various field offices will quite possibly range in size from multimillion-dollar operations in the larger metropolitan areas to the one- or two-person operations in the hamlets where you are trying to get established.

## McCAFFERTY'S LAW NUMBER TWO
### The service you are offering the customers must be available to them in their location.

At some point in your growth, this principle will require that larger offices be split into smaller offices to keep the services available to the customers. Customers in a state or particular defined geographic area prefer to be serviced from an office in their area, and sometimes have a dislike (which they will express to you at every opportunity) of being serviced out of an office in another state.

There are several ways to manage this as growth becomes a reality. One is to split an office into two or more parts as enough business becomes available in any particular part of the office territory. Let's say that Memphis has a field office with its own manager, and that its assigned territory is the western half of Tennessee and the state of Arkansas. You have a satellite office in Little Rock with a clerk and two or three service people. As soon as you can determine that there is enough business in Arkansas to make a split logical, the operation can be divided and a complete field office set up in Little Rock. This means a manager, separate reporting systems, salespeople, and the other requirements of a complete field office.

The usual problem is that we wait too long to make the split, thinking that there must be enough business there to completely support the additional management and administrative structure. The trick is to understand that as soon as a manager is assigned and given the responsibility for profit and growth and all those other things, the new office will start to grow very rapidly. The extremely rapid growth will be a result of having a manager in the locality, and of his being motivated to make his service business grow and prosper.

There's another way that is perhaps a bit more conservative but is just as effective. Put a supervisor in Little Rock and make him responsible for the performance of the business, reporting either to you or to your operations manager, if you have one. In other words, they have just become an official satellite rather than a mere remote office. Now get the necessary sales force in place in your new satellite, and have them report to your sales manager. You can have several of these satellites active and under the control of your office in Memphis. They will each be independent to a degree, and when they reach the size that you have established as a criterion, they can be cut loose as a full field office. The difference is that they have grown with a greater degree of control, while they were learning at the same time to be ready for their eventual independence.

This will give you an effective sales force throughout the entire territory, reporting to the sales manager, who reports to you. In each satellite the operations group is handled by a supervisor reporting to your operations manager, who reports to you. You have arranged, of course, for separate management and financial reporting for each office to allow you to monitor performance. They each have the benefit of your control until they are ready for independence, and they are very definitely in a training and learning climate. Again, the trick is to be sure to kick them out of the nest and put them on their own as soon as possible. Nothing will motivate them to grow faster than knowing that it is *their* service business and that *they* are responsible.

It is extremely important to build these remote operations into independent offices, and have your services available to the customers without their having either to pay for excessive travel or to wait for some service person to drive 200 miles to solve their problem. Although it is always a gamble to open a new office before it can be completely justified on a profit statement, the good businessman will go ahead when he knows it's not really a gamble, but a calculated risk. As with everything else, it takes commitment.

As your organization and the services you offer grow, they will of necessity become departmentalized and specialized. If you are servicing office equipment, you may develop separate departments for mechanical and electronic service. Service operations and sales are always naturals for a split. It is good sense to organize for the best effectiveness, and to ensure that each group with different needs will have them recognized. Be aware, though, of the need to maintain a cohesive identity.

Because of the newness of your organization, there will quite naturally be pressure to establish your organization along the same lines as other parts of the company, which may in reality be in altogether different areas of business.

Pay particular attention to the "span of effective management" concept, which states that any manager can manage only so many people effectively. The optimum is usually considered to be five to seven. This has a very real effect on your organization, in that you should be careful not to set up a field service office with the service people, clerical staff, salespeople, and field supervisors all reporting directly to the manager. As you develop a staff of your own, make sure that you don't have them all report directly. Organizations where everyone reports to the manager are extremely inflexible, particularly when the manager is unavailable. No one else has been trained to make the necessary decisions, nor does anyone feel responsibility for doing so, and as a result they are either not made at all or are made poorly.

The objective is to make the organization effective by allowing it to grow and to make money for you. Almost constant changes will be necessary to accomplish this. You will be able to make the changes much more acceptable to all if you are able to set things up in such a way that a particular part of the business that is growing much faster or that has the potential of much faster growth than the other parts of the business can be split off and allowed to go its own way to the greatest degree possible. After all, wasn't that how your service business got started in the first place—being split off from the rest of the company?

Another criterion for planning the future splitting off of a part of your service business is that one of your products or markets may be different from the others. It may require a completely different approach to the performance of service, a different method of planning and scheduling, or it may appeal to another kind of industry or customer. If you try to organize it the same way as your other groups, and leave it that way too long, it may be restricted in its growth because of being forced into a mold that doesn't fit its needs.

As people are given parts of your operation to manage, both the responsibility and the authority to run it properly must be delegated to them. Growth will inevitably create the need for front-line supervisors. As this starts to happen, their responsibilities must be structured around supervision rather than mere work direction. In this way they will be motivated to become the businessmen you need, not just hot-shot repairmen.

When designing your organization you need to con-

sider these and other matters which will later become
enormous problems if they are ignored. Although there
is no way that you can start off during the first week
with the organization you would like to have ten years
from now, you will be more likely to achieve those ultimate goals if you consider them carefully as you go
along. Everyone resists change to some degree, and
organizations as a whole resist change because they are
in reality nothing but a group of people. But the
changes will be resisted less if you structure the overall organization so that as each change occurs, it will
not be too drastic. Be careful, though: if ten years from
now someone outside your group sees one of your pre-
liminary sketches on organizational problems, you
could find yourself in hot water!

## PHYSICAL NEEDS

As your operation expands from an idea to a real-life
organization, you will need what is sometimes called
"physical plant." More often it is referred to as appropriation equipment, or perhaps capital appropriation
material. Each company handles it differently, and the
purchasing of such material will require specific procedures and a long string of approvals. Physical plant
includes such items as offices, furniture, communications systems, cars and trucks, and inventory. Another
item in this line is technical literature—not the printing
of it, but the distribution system and equipment.

Most of these things come to you almost automatically. The corporate real estate people find a building to suit your expressed needs, and buy or lease it
for you. A corporate office manager will examine charts
of how many square feet each person needs and of who

rates an office and who doesn't, and will come up with a list of furniture for you. The communication system will no doubt be preordained by the way your corporation already talks to its remote locations. Your need for cars and trucks will be handled normally by another part of the corporate structure that leases or buys vehicles. Someone will tell you the maximum inventory you are allowed to carry and will send it to you. Someone else will surely ask why you have so much of it.

The point is that although all these things and more are available through some part of your corporate structure, and getting them can sometimes be almost painless, it's important to be attentive. All of these corporate people are trying to help, and they will help to the extent of their capability. One of the more delightful things about being part of a large corporation is that you never feel alone: whatever strange situation you may fall into, there is always someone to help you extricate yourself. The difficulty is that these things will be provided to you in the normal manner in which all the other parts of the corporation have used them, but with no variations. Therefore you must assess all these things just to make sure they will do the job you want them to do. If you have a valid reason for following another procedure, there won't be too much difficulty in doing it your way. You just have to give your superiors a reason for proceeding in a manner that is obviously different from the way the company rules provide for.

As usual it's a matter of planning. You can easily get the facilities for the small number of employees you will be starting with in the new Podunk office, but try to arrange getting them in such a way that when the branch starts to grow, you don't have to change locations several times! Some things will be handled in a very routine manner, such as office furniture. But when it gets to communications, plan ahead to ensure that you will have the system and type of communications you require for the effective performance of your service function. Answering machines, recorders, data transmission, fax machines—all are common and relatively inexpensive for the work they do.

There is one thing you should keep in mind: the people in your corporate support groups will rarely have field service experience. If what you need is a truck, they will tend to get you the least expensive truck possible—even if it won't do the job you want it to do. It then falls upon your shoulders once again to communicate to them exactly what you want, why you want it, when you want it, and (as gently as possible) that they are after all buying or leasing the truck with your money.

### Tools and inventory

Tools are one of my own priorities. There are many who will try to save a dollar here and there, and I cannot find fault with anyone who tries to reduce cost. The use of cheap tools or the lack of proper tools, however, is one of the worst possible ways of effecting economy. In the service business, the thing you are selling is service, which really means people. Your service people are your primary asset, and they cannot be effective without the proper tools. Since any service people worth having take pride in their work, they must also be able to take pride in the tools they carry. And since they must use their time well to allow you to be profitable, they have to have the proper tools and instruments to do their jobs.

The situation is the same when you discuss the other

tools they will be using—cars, trucks, and so on. You will do well to get the best you can afford, and work it out in such a way that they have some choice in the type of vehicle, the manufacturer of their choice, or in the attachments and extras.

With regard to inventory, I can state with some certainty that there have been more books written on the subject than you can pack in one of your new service trucks. Suffice it to say that you need the material where the service people can get at it and can use it to the advantage of you and the customer. Distribution methods are effective enough these days that you need not stock each and every part in each office—the cost in inventory itself and the cost of maintaining it will be too high. But I would suggest that you stock in each location the parts and replacements that are common to many users, the ones that you may need for an emergency—to bail out your good customers on a Sunday morning, for example. The others, plus backup for all the material just mentioned, should be obtainable within hours from anywhere in the country, assuming that they are available in your distribution system and also assuming that you have made provision for rapid order handling and shipment (although making these two assumptions can often be dangerously misleading).

## BEWARE OF BUREAUCRACY

At all costs, keep your new business from developing a bureaucracy. It may not be a danger during the start-up period, but as you grow, and if there is both field and home office organization, your work will be cut out for you.

The simplest thing in the world is for a service manager from the field to be promoted to the home office or a region and to become so immersed in his work that he doesn't travel. After a year or so of this, his contact with day-to-day field operations may become remote. He remembers what he used to do in specific cases, but fails to realize that in the time he has been away from it things have changed. In this position of lofty omniscience, he decides that he knows very well what those people in the field need, and proceeds to give it to them. He is usually enraged when they make it painfully clear that they don't want it and that it won't work. Thus, a bureaucrat has been born.

The way to prevent this is to ensure that your home office management team makes periodic visits to the field, and that they take the time to study and analyze the day-to-day operations instead of spending all their field time talking to managers. As the organization grows, staff employees will begin to make routine decisions that will seriously affect field operations. Although it may at first appear to be a needless expense, it is worthwhile and a terrific investment to have these people make visits to field offices. That way you'll end up with fewer bureaucrats and more dedicated and effective employees.

As you build the home office staff, you will need to bring in some of your older and more experienced employees from the field. They are a very important asset because of their experience, and some of this is needed. In most cases, however, it is to your advantage to seek out younger employees who show real promise and bring them into the home office structure. Give them responsible jobs and let them learn to make decisions on a larger scale. From their overall view of your business, they will have a rare opportunity to see the things that field managers do—both the good and the bad.

They will be able to look at the entire operation and determine for themselves the differences between a successful office and an unsuccessful one.

After a few years of that kind of training, can you imagine a better source for the most effective managers available? But you have to expect possible opposition to your operating in this fashion: historically the procedure is to wait until managers are successful in the field and then rotate them to the home office to serve out their years in a position of greater responsibility.

When you announce new products or services, have your staff make the presentations at a meeting. Be sure they meet field people frequently at regional and area meetings, and that they represent you as often as possible. Each staff member should know each field manager personally, as well as some of the field employees in each office. If you can't make this work, then you have too many staff people. There must be enough people on your staff to do the necessary work, but a home office staff should always be a lean, hard-hitting organization.

Your staff must know they are there both to serve and to direct the field. If you keep them involved in field operations, they won't become bureaucrats.

# 3

## Planning for growth and setting goals and objectives

GROWTH IS POSSIBLE and can be accomplished almost to the degree you desire, but only if you plan for it. Planning for growth in an organization or a business is entirely different from, say, projecting utility costs for the next two years. There are basically two methods of planning—historical and growth. Both are very valid methods of charting the future when used in the proper manner.

### THE HISTORICAL PLANNING METHOD

The historical method is an intelligent extension of the past. It is saying that what you have done in the past you will do again, and to about the same degree. It is "extending the curve" as shown in Figure 2. If your growth in customer sales has been 5 percent per year through 1979, you can very easily forecast the same percentage of growth through the 1980s. This is a very

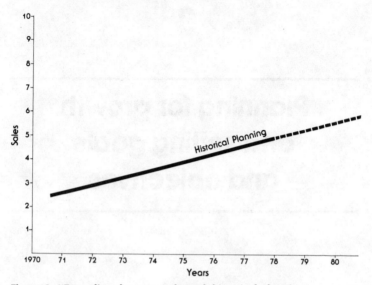

Figure 2. "Extending the curve" through historical planning.

simple method of planning the future, and is quite applicable to stable markets or costs.

Remember, though, that there is a very human tendency to be satisfied with performance against a plan. If you have planned to sell $200,000 worth of something in 1979, and have sold it by October, there is a tendency to relax a bit during the last two months of the year. One of the effects of historical planning is that you will tend to be satisfied with the same level of performance as in the past, and that may not really have been satisfactory. In cases where more of the same is quite sufficient, historical planning is simple and useful.

The historical planning concept seems most suitable to the more stable markets, almost I must state here that there are, or should be, very few stable markets. They should have enough stability so that they will still be there in a few years, but no market should be considered so stable that it cannot be made to grow faster.

If there is a single lonely customer somewhere buying a particular product or service of yours, you can find more if you take the trouble to locate and develop them. Again, historical planning is quite satisfactory for any market where you have agreed that past performance is satisfactory.

## GROWTH PLANNING

Growth planning is based on an entirely different concept—establishing a goal and then planning how you will get there from where you are. In planning sales, you must choose the point at which you would like to be in 1980 and extend the curve to that point (as shown in Figure 3). Here I must emphasize that the point selected for 1980 must *not* be where you will arrive

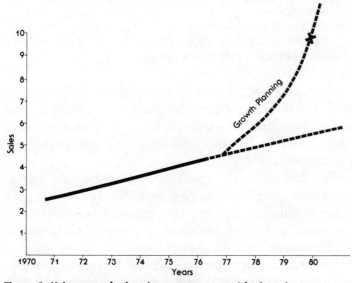

Figure 3. Using growth planning to target your ideal goal.

should you continue to do everything the same way, but the place you would be if all your hopes and dreams were to materialize. The goal has to be based on what you *want* to do.

When you extend the curve, plot the sales required for each year in between. The next step is to plan what you must do to get there from where you are. Perhaps there are several things required. This first time through, each of these must be plotted and calculated strictly on the basis of what must be provided to your organization to allow it to arrive at the final point, and not on the basis of resources that would normally be available. Let's say, for example, that these are the steps you must take between 1980 and 1985:

1. Develop a service sales force rather than depending on the customers to find you. This will also involve hiring, training, company cars, sales manuals, motivational programs, and many other aspects.
2. Expand your organization to 17 more cities. Hire more service people and provide them with trucks, tools, literature, and all their other needs.
3. Establish a training facility and the required training courses to train all these new people.

Now, let's look at some of the more detailed planning required to accomplish these goals. Developing a sales force from scratch is worth a book or two all by itself. Here are a few of the guideposts you will surely encounter along the way.

You'll need a sales manager from the outset—or at least very soon. You can do a lot of things yourself, but there are limits. And because this will become one of the most important positions in your organization, it requires somebody's full attention.

Next, you must establish policies to govern how the sales force will be paid, motivated, and rewarded. You must then determine how large the sales force will be to start and how much it will grow each year for the next five years.

Finally, there is a whole series of questions that you must answer: Where will the first salesperson you hire be located? Will he or she have a company car? How long will it take to get one? What about pricing manuals? And how about sales training? What will you teach him or her, and who will do it? How will you know whom to hire? Will there be sales material and brochures? Or sales contests? Or national sales meetings?

With regard to the expansion to 17 more cities, there will be as many questions, if not more. To select one need of the additional service person as an example, each one will need a vehicle of some kind. Let's say you have already decided upon vans as your standard vehicle. Under ideal conditions you will have the van fully equipped and sitting in the parking lot when the new service person returns from training school. Some of the procedures for accomplishing this might include purchasing or leasing the van itself, which may have to be planned considerably in advance because of anticipated delays in delivery. Then the van must be properly painted and marked with your corporate identity. It must be equipped with bins, drawers, and necessary cabinets to hold all the parts and material your service person will require, and the parts and material must be in them.

All of these steps must be taken in the proper sequence so that events will happen at the proper time. There are few things more costly than a service person or salesperson sitting in the office, unable to do the job because he or she doesn't have the tools. All of these things require planning, planning, and more planning. The secret of your job is planning and organization.

In real-life situations, there will of course be many

more tasks to accomplish. After you list them all, and you and your staff consider them, you may feel that within the structure of your company these tasks cannot all be accomplished within five years. The thing to do, then, is to move the target date back a year or two rather than lower your expectations on the objectives that must be accomplished. Ask yourself a question: now that the tasks are broken down into more manageable chunks, don't they seem more realistic and more practical to accomplish? Once your sights are set and the intermediate steps are detailed, it is merely a matter of first convincing yourself that accomplishment is possible and then convincing your management that the entire plan is feasible.

If this is the first time a real topnotch growth plan has been presented to your management, you should be prepared for your bosses to react as if you are crazy! Remember that they are not used to this sort of plan, so their reactions should not be considered unreasonable. After all, you are coming on strong as a dreamer, an entrepreneur, and a person with a sense of mission.

Naturally you have to explain all of the details to them in their terms, but the most important point you can make to them is that if they want the results you have outlined (that enormous sales number in 1985), they will have to provide the support you have outlined. Be aware that this commitment on their part must be long term. As the years go by, things will change within the company, people will change, and their ideas will change. If you are able to perform according to the plan, you will have to regain their full commitment every year. (A word of advice here: When it comes time for all departments in your company to submit their growth plans—and when some of them have had bad years—be careful about how you communicate your own ambitious, optimistic plans. Trumpeting your own successes and dreams of future glory may rub people the wrong way and may leave a bad taste in their mouths. Don't broadcast your plans until the meeting, and make sure to get yourself scheduled last on the program.)

During these growth years (and all your years can be growth years) it will be an absolute necessity for you to plan and accomplish the goals you have set for yourself and your organization. Attainment of the magic point on the curve for 1985 is entirely possible. It *can* be done! But the planning must be constant, and you must always know where you are going and what you must do to get there—not only for your own day-to-day actions, but to allow you to answer the continuing (but completely justified) questions of management and your peers.

This is where the sense of mission comes in. When you propose this degree of growth, and everyone says you're mad, but you really do it—that's a feeling of accomplishment that just can't be beat. It's like building the tallest building, the longest bridge, or circumnavigating the globe in a canoe: it's impossible, but you did it!

## MAINTAINING GROWTH

Maintaining growth at the desired rate will always be difficult. This is true because of the difficulty in sustaining a high level of performance year in and year out. It's also true because your markets—the specific services you sell to your customers—have a tendency to level off after a few years and to become stabilized.

This leveling has many causes. For example, let us assume that the first service you sold to customers was "call" service, in that when the customer called and requested service, you performed the service required and then charged the customer. A few years later, you also began to sell the customers parts over the counter in your various offices. (We'll call this service "parts.") At some later date you began a program of contract preventive maintenance for a fixed fee per year. (We'll call this service "contract.") Although this year you are putting more of your effort into selling "contract," you are still selling "call" and "parts."

The growth in each of these markets will have a tendency to flatten and become more stable as the years go on and as other more saleable markets become established. As you can see in Figure 4, each of your markets

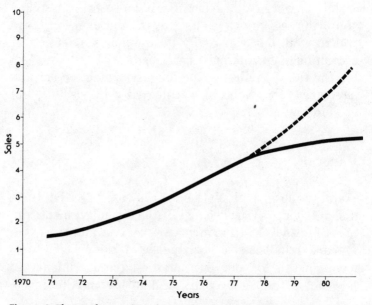

Figure 4. The tendency of markets to level out over time.

will have a tendency to grow initially and then level off as more emphasis is put on your other activities. Remember that if you maintain the emphasis on each of the markets as the years go on, they need not level off. This will take some watching on your part, since it is quite natural to pay less attention to the old "bread and butter" programs when more interesting and glamorous products become available.

To provide the growth that you targeted for 1985, you may find it necessary to constantly add new products, new services, and new variations on the old ones. In this way you can satisfy the requirements of your salespeople, who need a shot in the arm now and then while you are expanding the scope of your business. You can see in Figure 5 what effect this can have on your business as the years go on.

Even when they flatten out and stabilize, your mar-

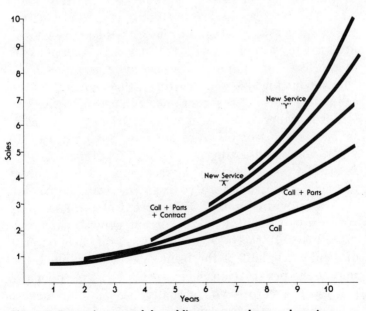

**Figure 5. Promoting growth by adding new products and services.**

kets will tend to reinforce each other and push you closer and closer to that goal you set some years back. As these events start to occur, you will find out whether you set the goal high enough in the first place. One thing you must watch for: whenever you are successful in creating a new business, you must of course exploit it. If you don't watch it, you'll be so busy keeping your past promises that you won't have time left to do anything creative or new and different. If that happens to you—if you ever allow yourself to lose your drive, your sense of mission, or your creativity—your business will stagnate in a very short time.

## CONSEQUENCES OF GROWTH

Assuming that you are now growing within the limits of your plan, you will start to notice some important effects of that growth. For one thing, your status within the company will change on the basis of how fast you are growing compared with the rest of the company. If at the birth of your business we make some assumptions about the size and growth of the segments of the company, some interesting things will become apparent.

For instance, if we assume that at the start the company has sales of 50 units and you have sales of 10 units, you are starting out with 16.7 percent of total sales. If we also assume 5 percent growth for the rest of the company and 15 percent for you, within ten years you will represent 33.2 percent of total sales. If you were to maintain a 20 percent growth rate each year, after 12 years you will represent 49.8 percent of total sales, half of the total sales! (In Table 1 you can see the progression each year: it won't be too many more years before you actually become the largest sales unit in the entire company.)

**Table 1. Comparing the growth rate of the service business to that of the company as a whole.**

| Year | Unit Sales of Rest of Company | Unit Sales of Service Business at Growth Rate of | | Percentage of Total Sales at Growth Rate of | |
|---|---|---|---|---|---|
| | | 15% | 20% | 15% | 20% |
| Start | 50 | 10 | 10 | 16.7 | 16.7 |
| 1 | 52.5 | 11.5 | 12 | 18.0 | 18:6 |
| 2 | 55.1 | 13.2 | 14.4 | 19.3 | 20.7 |
| 3 | 57.9 | 15.2 | 17.3 | 20.8 | 23.0 |
| 4 | 60.8 | 17.5 | 20.7 | 22.3 | 25.4 |
| 5 | 63.8 | 20.1 | 24.9 | 24.0 | 28.1 |
| 6 | 67.0 | 23.1 | 29.9 | 25.6 | 30.9 |
| 7 | 70.3 | 26.6 | 35.8 | 27.5 | 33.7 |
| 8 | 73.9 | 30.6 | 43.0 | 29.3 | 36.8 |
| 9 | 77.6 | 35.2 | 51.6 | 31.2 | 39.9 |
| 10 | 81.4 | 40.5 | 61.9 | 33.2 | 43.2 |
| 11 | 85.5 | 46.6 | 74.3 | 35.3 | 46.9 |
| 12 | 89.8 | 53.6 | 89.2 | 37.4 | 49.8 |

As you can imagine, the effect of this will be that your status within the company will change considerably. Those who at the start considered you to be small and insignificant will begin to realize that your organization is now of considerable importance. Various support groups (such as training, accounting, personnel, and publications) will have to reconsider their priorities in scheduling your work through their departments. You will be invited to meetings that you never attended before. You will be asked for more input at planning time and you will have more responsibility for the continued success of the company.

These changes will happen gradually in most cases. But as they do take place throughout the years, you will be faced with a new problem: you will have to struggle to maintain the identity of your service business. People who initially believed that you couldn't possibly make a success of the service business, and that it should remain a free sales tool, will begin to realize that you are now a thriving part of the company. Attempts will be made to absorb your business into other departments. After all, you can't blame people for wanting to be involved with a winner, can you?

When these things start to happen, you must ask yourself whether the suggested changes are good for the service business and for the company as a whole. Will they help accomplish your long-range plans, or will they just get in the way? Will they dilute the effectiveness of the company's efforts to provide service to customers? If the service organization were to lose its identity, would it also lose its effectiveness?

You must have the answers to these questions ready, and be prepared to discuss them with your management, for as surely as the sun rises the questions will be asked and the reorganizations will be suggested. There will also be continuing external pressure for change, pressure that originates in the world outside the service business and the company. Primarily it will come from customers who are responding to their changing needs and desires.

And that raises another central point: as the customers change, you must change. Only to a degree can you dictate to customers what they need and want, and how they will get it. This brings us to two more of McCafferty's Laws.

## McCAFFERTY'S LAW NUMBER THREE
The successful service business will be the one that delivers to its customers the services they need and want.

## McCAFFERTY'S LAW NUMBER FOUR
Should customers not fully understand their needs and wants, it is your responsibility to explain them.

Companies that continue to sell outmoded products and services are outmoded themselves. To survive in a world of change, you have to change yourself!

## FINANCIAL MODELS: THE THREE-YEAR PLAN

In Chapter 1 mention was made of financial models. One of the best things you can possibly do is to keep a financial model at all times. One way to do this is to require each part of your service business to submit a three-year operational plan each year. In addition, you as the manager will maintain a five-year plan. This will demand time and effort, but it will be well worth it.

The three-year plan should be based on the same measurements as your regular profit and loss statements and cost reports, but the forms should be revised somewhat to allow for growth over the three-year period. There should also be allowance in the format of your three-year plan for the trends that will be emerging. As the plan is developed for each operating unit, it will be your responsibility to combine them to develop regional and national plans.

When you initiate the three-year planning concept and announce it to your field organization, there will probably be a great hue and cry. Your field people will feel that a three-year plan based on the hoped-for growth will be converted into required *normal* performance. To put it another way, the hoped-for growth projected in the three-year plan will become a "floor" for measuring actual performance, not a "ceiling" for delineating optimal achievement. They fear that this will force them to plan the steps required to support this hoped-for growth and that when they do as you ask (which to them will include some rather far-out planning), you will then require them to accomplish it as routine performance.

To counter this criticism, you should explain to them that the three-year plan was developed as a completely separate entity from the annual financial planning cycle, and has even been scheduled for a different time of year. Reassure them that your purpose is to plan long range to demonstrate what kind of growth is possible and to stretch their imaginations a bit. All of these statements are true, and will ring with sincerity as you say them. In fact, they are the real reasons you developed the three-year planning system in the first place, so you are not in any way trying to sell them a bill of goods.

After you have actually gone through the three-year cycle several times, you will begin to see what is really possible if you try hard enough and have the necessary support. Then you will notice a new trend developing in your business—matching the three-year plan's "Gee, if we could only make this happen" and the real performance of each year. Thus, you will have a tendency to expect the better performance developed by the planning techniques. Their suspicions will be confirmed, and they will even realize themselves that it is a justifiable expectation.

The point is that the performance you would *like* to see each year is possible: With planning and support it can be done. The standard reason for planning is to project what will happen for the next period of time, usually a year, so that the people running the company will know where they are going. The other, less common reason for planning is that by the process of planning in the proper manner, you can see where it is possible to go, and will therefore have more of a tendency to get there because you know that it *is* possible.

## SETTING GOALS AND OBJECTIVES

In Chapter 1, we discussed the setting of goals and objectives related mostly to the initial establishment of your service business. In reality, you will need to set goals and objectives as long as you are in any business at all.

Before we continue we should define these two things that will play such a large part in our lives. According to the dictionaries, they are somewhat the same: "that toward which effort is directed." For our purposes, however, an objective is a task to be accomplished by a specific time, usually a year or less. A goal is something to be accomplished over a longer period of time, and is more important. For example, an objective might be to hire a new technician within 30 days, whereas a goal would be to develop a well-trained technical force within two years.

As you start to set goals and objectives for your new business, you'll notice that you are to a degree exploring virgin territory. Not that this hasn't been done before for a new business (it has been), but it's probably new to you, and since you are starting a new business it's certainly new to your company. Within your company, people have gone through this before, but not for a new service business. Since the service business is different from the "regular" business of your company, the goals and objectives will vary from what you are all used to.

For one thing, you are setting your goals on the basis of considerable growth, and the objectives of your people and yourself will be largely directed toward accomplishing that growth. This means that those who are charged with approving what you do will take some convincing before they will endorse your plans. In effect you are changing the charter of the company, or at least that of the part of the company to which you are reporting.

You will no doubt become familiar with the words, "But we never did it that way before." The best answer to this statement is that if what we did worked well before and if it still works, we'll keep doing it. If it doesn't work any more, we'll do it differently. Attitudes such as these have a tendency to brand you as a maverick, and as one who does not have the proper respect for tradition. But if you intend to be the entrepreneur and innovator that you must be in order to succeed in a new venture, you must learn not to worry about what people may call you.

The easiest mistake in the establishment of a new venture is to underestimate by a large degree the time needed to build a business from scratch (see Figure 1). If you are to be allowed any control at all of the initial timing of the goal and of the objective setting, give yourself enough time to get the task accomplished, because the start-up pains can be terrible. It's one thing to have to hire another technician, but it's quite another to hire one when you do not even have the forms available from your personnel department to put him on the payroll. It's one thing to hire a typist, but it's another thing entirely when you have the typist but have not yet had the opportunity to purchase a typewriter, paper, and a chair and a desk for him or her to sit at. These are the start-up problems that are rarely planned for, since the planners are removed from such details of operation—and have been for many years.

If you start your new business in an established location, add a few people at a time, and have all the usual corporate backup at your disposal, it's a relatively simple job. But if you are directed to move your family to another city, find a building and lease it, hire the people you need, start the business, and have it producing in a month or so, then the going will be rougher. It's not only difficult to accomplish all those things at once; it's virtually impossible without a considerable amount of advance planning. If your objectives for the year include this sort of a start, you will need to spend some time with your boss discussing what the objectives should really be, and what the consequences will be if those objectives are not met to the letter.

After the start-up come the growing pains, which also need continuing attention. The difference is that by the time you have growing pains you have probably found out what to do and how to do it, and you must only figure out how to do more of it in less time—or how to do it better. It's a period of getting the bugs out of your original plan and of refining your procedures and policies.

Something else can very easily happen at the start: since the rest of your company will be expecting results from your efforts—and customers may also be hoping for something—don't get carried away with promises. In the planning stages, allow for the time it will take you to set up, to hire people, to train and equip them, and to make them available to do their work. In your planning, allow for the things that will go wrong, the contingencies you won't anticipate, and the ideas that just won't work. Of course you can't plan for each one in detail, since you won't be able to identify some of these terrible situations until they happen. But you can plan for the worst situation and allow for time and for what your management will consider to be the unreasonable expenditure of funds to correct the problems.

In setting long-range goals, one of the major problems seems to be focusing on the primary target—how big do we plan to be ten years from now? At this point you should set your sights on how big you *want* to be: You can be as big as you wish, just as long as you put in the required effort, imagination, and financing, and make the necessary commitments.

It sounds so simple to say that you can be as big as you wish, but one thing that must happen is the introduction of realism into the process of planning and setting of goals and objectives. One danger is that you will acquiesce to those who are unfamiliar with the process of growth planning, and that you will set your sights too low. It's also dangerous to set them so high that they cannot possibly be attained.

Let's say that you have gone through the steps of planning your service business as a cost center, and that your financial people say you will be able to turn the corner into profitability in 3½ years. Let's also suppose that this timing is based on the very conservative outlook of the financial staff. Now is the time for you to look at it as the dreamer, the entrepreneur, the person with the mission whom we have been talking about. You have to go again through the entire plan and look at each item, asking yourself some very important questions—the "what if . . ." questions:

◻ What if we hired seven salespeople instead of four?
◻ What if we were to have three training classes for service people each year instead of one?
◻ What if we were to increase our pricing structure by 5 percent?
◻ What if we were able to reduce our overall cost by 3 percent?
◻ What if we were to purchase cars and trucks locally for the first two years, to eliminate the wait for our leasing agent to get vehicles?

You must ask yourself all these questions (or those that apply to your situation) and many more. Do not accept the word of the "others" as final; ask yourself the questions that may at first seem ridiculous, since by asking them you may get a few new ideas for actions that you can take to affect the outcome. There is *always* something you can do to affect the outcome. The primary ingredients in finally setting the goals and objectives are imagination and commitment.

As you start on a small scale, there will be a small budget and many things you will not be able to afford until next year. If you start big, there will be the problem of bureaucracy, but chances are that your starting size will be dictated by the needs of the business as you see it rather than being an arbitrary size chosen only for the sake of making a decision. The state of the business on the day the decision is made to enter the service business will determine whether you are to start in a city or a region, whether you will go national, and what services you will offer at first. Your responsibility is then to take that initial decision—molded from the cries of wounded customers—and mold it further so it will give you, over a period of time, the business you want.

# 4

---

# Where
# does the money
# come from?

---

THERE IS only one realistic answer to the question, "Where does the money come from?": it comes from the customers. This is one of the problems of business, although it is more obvious in large corporations than in small companies. A company can be said to consist of two kinds of organizations, field and support. The field groups are those that meet the customers nose to nose, and are usually the sales, service, and installation or start-up groups. The others are support groups—training, personnel, accounting, office services, ware-housing and distribution, marketing, and so on. Although there is always a normal amount of rivalry between such groups, the trouble starts when one of them gets the idea that *it* really makes the money that all the other groups in the company merely spend. McCafferty's Law Number Five should dispel that notion:

## McCAFFERTY'S LAW NUMBER FIVE
### The only real source of money is customers.

But how do you get this money that came from the customers? When the company gets it from the customers, it isn't passed out evenly among the employees; it goes to the accounting department, and from that time, you must act properly if you want any of it. It doesn't matter if you call it budgeting, planning, or financial reporting. Whatever you call it, the accounting department gets it, and if you want some you will have to give the money people a good reason why they should give it to you instead of to some other project, or even to the stockholders

The individual in charge of all this is usually called a comptroller. As a group, comptrollers take a dim view of the visionary entrepreneur after whom we have been modeling ourselves. Comptrollers have a tendency to put the money in a safer place where it may not earn as much but where the return (in their opinion) is more certain. It is therefore your job to convince this person that instead of fighting you over it, he should give it up to you willingly, since he is after all investing in the most growth-oriented group in the corporation!


## FINANCING THE OPERATION AND DEALING WITH ACCOUNTING PEOPLE

The most basic financial matter of all is how your operation is to be financed. If you are to be a cost center, what kind of cost? Will you operate on a budget from the sales department? The production department? How will your budget be established? What approval chain do you have? Is the objective to maintain cost

within a specific budget, or is it to provide zero profit?
If you are not given a budget, do you operate on a percentage of sales? If you are to be a profit center, how
much profit? How are your overheads calculated? Are
they specific costs or allocations? Are some of your
costs part of a "pool" for several departments? Are
you charged for costs that arise from the activities of
other departments?

Many times the accounting procedures for a new service operation will necessarily be very basic in the
initial stages. After all, if you are a $100,000 operation
within a multimillion-dollar corporation, you can't expect your own accounting department. But as you get
to be a multimillion-dollar operation yourself, your
needs change.

The most difficult thing is for the accounting procedures to keep pace with the growth of the business.
There are reasons why accounting practices change
slowly. The outside accountants, the Internal Revenue
Service, and the stockholders take an understandably
dim view of your changing the basic reporting system
of your company every year—it can even give them
the impression that you are trying to conceal something. Also, these days your accounting is done largely
by a computer, and you should be aware of the fact
that complicated computer programs cannot be
changed overnight (or even over an entire year, sometimes). There are also a lot of other reasons that any
accountant worth his salt can give you for not changing
things. It has been my personal experience, however,
that accounting departments build in a resistance to
change that is based as much on the difficulty of making
the change as it is on the needs of the service operation.
It therefore becomes your responsibility to persuade
them of the need and the value of the change and to

negotiate a constantly improving system of financial reporting that will serve your changing business.

One of your first tasks in dealing with finance and accounting people is to learn to speak their language, since the odds are good that they will not be too interested in using your language. Become conversant in their terms: ROI, ROA, and so on. Although you may not initially have to understand all that is said in the corporate annual statement, you should understand how the information gets translated from a divisional operating statement to the corporate "top books" and from there to the annual statement to the stockholders. Each group involved in the numbers has a different informational need, which requires that the numbers be stated differently.

As your operation develops, another problem will surface. As each segment of the division makes a profit, that revenue is apportioned to the entire division as is necessary to meet their operating costs and to finance their growth—and of course, that inevitable percentage goes to the corporation for its costs. It is your responsibility, as it is of all operating managers, to try to retain as much of your profit as possible to finance your own growth. This will take a bit of doing, but realizing that you have to get in there and fight for it is half the battle.

## KEEPING TRACK OF YOUR COSTS

In the initial years, the easiest way to set up the accounting of your costs is to ally yourself financially with a similar part of the organization, possibly the one from which you split off. This means that although your sales and a few of the primary costs will be very carefully separated, many of your indirect and overhead costs will be pooled with those of the other group and allocated accordingly.

For example, let's assume that both of your groups purchase tools, and that these have traditionally been reported as a separate line in cost reporting by the parent group. Now that you have become a separate entity, the simplest accounting procedure is to have both of you purchase tools in the same account. Then, on the basis of some related activity such as headcount (how many people each of you has in the categories that use tools) or possibly sales, the costs would be allocated to each of you as a percentage of the total.

This procedure works quite smoothly, and has the advantage of being rather simple for the accounting department. Its disadvantage is that it is unfair to both departments whenever one of you gets bigger than the other. If your tools are generally more expensive than those used by the other group, it's unfair to them. Since the group with the most people (if that's the basis for determining allocations) will always pay the largest percentage of the cost, the group with the fewest people soon learns to take advantage of the allocation system, and that's unfair.

This may be a way to get started, but as soon as you can muster enough horsepower—even if you are winning the allocation game—get the cost accounting split off from the pool concept. Although you will in some cases pay more than you did under pool costing, you will be surprised how many times you will pay less. Not only that, but the name of the game in the service business is to identify each and every cost you have, mark it up by the appropriate amount to establish your pricing base, and then mark *that* up for the desired profit. You can do this correctly only when you know what the costs really are.

As part of the structure of a large corporation, you

may sometimes find it extremely difficult to sort out your costs from those of the other groups and then to identify them exactly It will take extreme effort on your part, and corresponding effort on the part of the accounting and computer departments. What it will really require is untiring effort in finding reported items that you do not understand, and bringing them to the attention of those who can change the system.

It will also be necessary for you to make your people aware of the problem. One way to do this is to take one input document (a service report with both labor and material, to be billed to a customer, for example) and track it all the way through the system from start to finish. I mean *all* the way—through each and every person handling it, and monitoring what they do and why they do it; looking at every computer printout that has any details deriving from this document, and following them through each and every person, and seeing what steps they take. This is the only way to determine how things go astray, why your sales were off last month, why your inventory doesn't make sense, and so on. It takes time and effort, and may not make you too many friends in the accounting end of the house (depending on how tactfully you do it), but it is the only way and it is your responsibility.

In most large companies there are so many steps involved in the paperwork for a single transaction that your detective work on what really happens to things may take some time, and should perhaps proceed in steps. For example, you could start with the entering of a customer order for service: What happens to it? Who accepts the order? Is it handled differently by telephone than it is by mail? What form is used to transcribe the order? Who does it? Who makes the decision about what priority will be assigned to the service call? How does the information on the call get transmitted to the service person?

If you then assume that the service person performs the work and completes his service report, what happens to that? How is the material used removed from your inventory? How does the customer get billed, and who calculates the final amount? Who figures the tax? How does your Omaha office get credit for the work it does, and what happens to all the charges and credits when the Sioux Falls office takes a call in Omaha's territory? From this rather brief list of questions you can see many possible audit trails to follow.

In the long run these kinds of audits must be performed periodically on each and every kind of transaction you handle in your system. Of course, you can request that your accounting department make the audits, although they will probably avoid doing so, since it is time-consuming and expensive. It is also true that it will put them in the position of auditing their own performance and reporting on it, which is not the best way to get a completely candid audit. For it to be really effective, you must perform the audit with your people. You are the user of the services, it is your financial statement that will be affected, and it is your customers who are being billed. Therefore you have the responsibility, as usual. Since you will never have the time to audit everything at once without driving everyone mad, do a document or a transaction each year. When you get big enough, put an operational auditor on the payroll. You'll no doubt have a struggle proving that you need one, but by then you will be an expert at proving that sort of thing to management.

# 5

# Records and reports

THERE ARE three basic purposes to a reporting system: management, operations, and financial. I'll discuss each one in turn.

*Management* reporting tries to develop the big picture, for those who need to observe and control the direction of the total business. It needs to report only the significant information, such as sales, cost, overhead, and profit. There is also a need to report the "alarm" information, the things that may cause trouble if they go wrong. These "alarm" details will normally vary from time to time as different parts of the business become more or less significant.

*Operations* reporting is for the people who maintain day-to-day and week-to-week control of the business. It is usually much more detailed, with breakdowns of all the factors they must be aware of in order to manage properly.

*Financial* reporting is for the divisional and corporate people who are interested in financing, return on investment, and the relationships between the various parts of the company. These will normally be the comptroller, the accountants, the vice-presidents, and the department heads.

The informational needs of these different groups vary widely and must be stated in different terms. In may cases the information going to one group will not be too easily understood by the others. To ensure the success of the business we must ensure that the reporting of it is in the language of those who are reading the reports.

One of our persistent problems is that reporting systems are designed by the accounting and data processing departments. Although their intentions are always the best, they have a tendency to structure the reports in such a way that they will be most easily understood by themselves and in such a manner that they can most easily collect the information from already existing systems and reports. For example, if we assume that the service business is new to your company and that you have been in manufacturing for years, the odds are good that your first reporting systems will be structured around existing factory systems. Although the information at the end of the line may very well be adequate for the financial people, it may be in terms that will be difficult for your operating people to understand, and in management terms that do not relate to the service business. The difficulty is that once the systems are in place, it will take years of negotiation to get them changed.

If you are a new service business, it is to your advantage to get involved at the start in developing reporting systems tailored to your needs in the operating and management areas, and which will properly convert to the financial systems of the company. This way all parties involved can get what they need. But you must understand the business well enough to design a reporting system and be able to communicate your needs to the accounting and data processing groups clearly enough so that they will devise the system you need.

Getting your field people involved is of the greatest importance. If regional and local office management people will have to use the system, and will be judged on the output of the system, they must have a part in its development and in what will be constant and continual refinements. It just isn't fair and honest to fire a manager for nonperformance when the basis of his or her performance is a system of reports that neither of you can understand, and that neither of you really has faith in.

## INFORMATIONAL NEEDS AS DETERMINED BY POSITION AND LOCATION

Informational needs also vary in another way—by the action or reaction that people in the organization are expected to take as a result of their reading the reports. In this respect it's not so much a matter of whether they are included in management, operations, or financial, but where they are located—both organizationally and geographically.

*Field* people, including service people, the clerical staff, and the stockroom people, will be given certain specific information from the system, and on that basis they will be expected to perform their tasks more effectively and to operate within certain rules. The information they get must be planned in such a way that it illuminates the area of their responsibility.

*Field management* requires the detailed operational information to allow it to perform effectively, and to manage the business on a day-to-day basis. Over a period of time these people will also need the larger picture, since it will help them to understand where they are going. There is no better way to make field managers less effective than to withhold information from them on the theory that "you'll tell them what *they* need to know."

The *staff,* which includes the regional and home office staff people, needs all the information the other parts of the organization get so it can monitor what's going on. But staff people will also need something more: the information that will help them observe the effects of changes, the activity of specific markets, and the effectiveness of programs in progress.

*Top management* people need the detail they ask for, which may vary from time to time as they zero in on one problem or another. They also need reporting by exception (see discussion later in chapter), alarms, what has gone outside some specified limit, what has gone wrong somewhere, what will be a cause of trouble next week and next month—and next year.

There is also a question about the difference in information needed for you to survive or prosper. You can survive on very basic information and even on late, inaccurate, and somewhat incomprehensible data. To prosper, however, you need information that is current and accurate.

## USING COMPUTER SYSTEMS

At some point someone will say that life would be so much easier were you to put everything on a computer. And it would be—assuming that it all worked.

## McCAFFERTY'S LAW NUMBER SIX
### Before you ever agree to put anything on a computer, make sure it works!

These days you can put anything on a computer. The point is that if your paperwork system will not work manually, it won't work in the machine either. Once it's in the machine it's harder to make changes and adjustments, so if you have a choice, get it working first.

From the point of view of a user of computer systems, some simple and some very complicated, there are a few guidelines to follow.

1. Set your system up for manual operation, but always keep in mind that at some point in the future you'll be using a computer. This way you can always be looking to the future and planning which parts of the system will work best on the machine, which parts should remain manual, and the reason for each decision.

2. When you are operating manually, count everything. Although you may not need to know how many green forms you handle every day for any business reason, you will need to know the volume and frequency of each kind of paperwork when you start designing a system.

3. Be sure that someone on your staff spends a lot of time thinking about how you process the paperwork. It goes from one work station to another, but in what order and why? Is there a reason for each step? Is there a better way? Why on earth do you need that second file copy?

4. When it's time to start talking to computer people, you must make sure that you and the members of your staff are involved in the system design from start to finish. At each point you must meet with the data processing group and approve each detail of the sys-

tem design. Data processors will design a system on the basis of their view as observers of your system. Their view of your system will be based on looking at the paperwork, talking to other related departments, and some visits to your area. Their intentions will be the best, but their time will be limited, so you must take the time to make sure that they understand from the user's point of view how the business really works.

5. It is unbelievably simple to get a report from a computer. The real problem is to keep from getting too many reports. Since a computer can calculate things so simply, the computer people will create all kinds of exciting reports. For example, if you are in the business of manufacturing and servicing toasters, you may be very interested in how many units of each model were shipped in the last month. You may not care too much how many were shipped on Tuesday afternoons, but if the data is in the computer, someone is sure to suggest that it be included in one of the printouts.

Your task in this area is to go through every report and to scrutinize it in detail to determine if the report includes the information you want, if it includes any information you don't want, and if it calls things by their proper names. If your people in the field identify a particular report line as "truck cost," be sure that is the way they identify it in the report: there is always a possibility that it will be called "distributed vehicle expenditures."

6. Data processing staffs, like the rest of us, have a tendency to run out of budget money before a project is complete. When this happens, they will no doubt explain to you that although each detail of your system is not complete, it is essentially working, and you should be agreeable and certify the project as complete. They will promise to complete the final details

later and will urge you not to worry about it. Don't believe them! Sign for only what you did get, and explain in writing and in detail the parts that are not complete. In addition, get some written agreement as to when they will be complete.

7. When the system is in the test phase, be personally involved in the testing. Too often a test will be satisfactory to the data processing group, but not to the user. Be sure that you see each option exercised, and that you see the expected results.

## MANAGEMENT BY DETAIL AND BY EXCEPTION

Believe it or not, your management style will be the result of the reports you get. There are two basic ways to monitor a business: by detail and by exception. To monitor by detail, you amass reports of every number the accountants can come up with, and have them displayed several ways. From this you also create summaries. Each month you analyze the full spectrum of reports and make the necessary business decisions (that is, you make the decisions if you have any time left over from analyzing the reports). If you operate in this manner, you will have no doubts about what is going on; it is just a matter of separating the essentials from the mass of superfluous material. You may very well decide to start this way until you find out what does happen every month and become familiar with the trends. At that point, you can get the accounting and reporting changed to meet your needs.

Once you have mastered all this, you will be ready for management by exception. In its simplest form, this means that the only things reported to you are the exceptions. In other words, the only time the system tells you anything is when something goes wrong. The rest of the time you assume that all is well. For this to work you need several things: an accounting and reporting system that has been proved to work properly; a dependable computer system; a relatively stable business, meaning that you're out of the start-up stage and are running smoothly; and faith, a calm demeanor, and a lot of courage.

Should you ever get to the point of management by exception, you can be sure that you will not be bothered by a ton of reports to read every month, but if something goes wrong, you'll be notified right away. If you and your management are not quite ready for this, take the intermediate step of adding trend reporting to your "full detail" reports. As you identify a few of the trends that are most liable to affect your business, you can begin to dispense with some of the detail. As soon as you start doing that, you'll be managing by exception in a few more years.

Another thing that should be mentioned here is that with manual files, your search for any particular piece of data is limited only by how long it takes to go through enough files to find it. With the proper computer system, you can proceed from one level of detail to the next until you reach the data you require. One example would be tracking down how the labor cost on a specific service call was established. It could work like this: you ask your computer terminal for the proper field office by number. When you ask for labor costs, it displays the applicable labor accounts. When you select the proper account number for service contract labor, it displays all the charges to that account during the last month. When you ask for a specific week, it displays those charges. When you enter the service order number, it displays the service report detail, the name and Social Security number of the service person, the hours worked, and whatever other data is available. You get the information you ask for at each level and in the detail you require.

Have you ever had the opportunity to observe how the airline reservation systems work? At the first level, you punch in the city of destination and the computer reacts by displaying all appropriate flight numbers. When you punch in one of the flight numbers, you see the schedule, the kind of equipment, the prices, how many seats, and so on. Then, when you ask for available space, it displays what seats are open. At each level of information, you can ask a question and proceed to the next level of detail.

I'm not trying to convince you of the need for a fancy computer system, but as your business becomes more complicated and sophisticated, you will have to do something to keep from being buried in information. It takes more skill as a manager to manage by trend and exception, but by the time you need the systems you'll have the skills. You must balance the cost of computerizing against the cost of having to wait to find out what's happening. In these days of constant change, it's absolutely essential for you to know what's going on daily or even hourly.

If used properly, computers can give you something more than the regular and sometimes frightening supply of reports and schedules. Once you are on a computer, and the manner in which you perform your business has been programmed into it, your expertise is "in the machine." If you think hard enough, and have a good systems analyst at your side, you can develop better ways to operate the business. Today, even smaller computers have an astonishing capacity to collect and report information, and this will allow you to print out the valuable expertise and examine it in an organized way for perhaps the first time ever. Of course, you will be able to perform such tasks as analyzing costs, but you will also be able to analyze completely the manner in which you perform your services, the tasks your service people perform, and the steps your salespeople must follow to develop sales leads. The potential for evaluating and improving your business is staggering.

# 6

# Building a field manager: Selection

EVERYONE is proud of growth. Along with the compliments and monetary rewards you get the pleasure of anticipating the day when you can sit back and watch the business run itself. But that won't happen—ever. An organization must always be managed, and that requires managers, which in turn requires the selection and building of managers.

The word "building" is used intentionally. A manager is not just hired or promoted into a position and taught a job; he is built, trained, developed, and nurtured. It has been said that the true test of a manager is not just his sales volume, but how many good people he has developed and whom the company has been able to place in more responsible positions. The primary job is developing people. If you succeed at that, you automatically develop the business.

Growth places greater demands on managers and on those who must acquire, build, and unfortunately sometimes replace them. With growth comes change—in the volume of activities to be managed, in procedures, policies, equipment, and people. Unmanaged change is chaos.

Even if a company were able to survive with zero growth, change is inevitable. The Model T had its effect on the buggywhip industry, the development of aircraft changed the railroads and ship lines, vaudeville was eclipsed by the movies, and the service industry is being changed by consumerism and many other forces.

Internal changes are inevitable: a reshuffling of divisions; a new vice-president with new ideas; you're suddenly a profit center instead of a sales cost; the company creates a new division and you're in it—or out of it. And then there are technical changes. Products, materials, and methods becomes obsolete, and the manager who is tied to the old products also becomes obsolete. Like the home the family has outgrown, he must be remodeled or replaced. Some managers can anticipate their own futures and adapt to them, or can perceive their own changing needs and find their own answers. Most cannot, at least not without encouragement and guidance.

These factors, plus normal attrition rates, help ensure that the building of field managers will continue to be a top priority job. Unfortunately, it's a job most of us are inadequately prepared for. We know more about the requirements for a technician than for a good field manager. We fill positions instead of developing people. We reach for the good salesperson and shove him or her into the manager's slot, and thereby trade a good salesperson for a mediocre manager or a competent technician for an incompetent manager.

If we fail to react rationally to change in this vitally

important area, we cease to be managers and instead become victims. The more day-to-day problems we have to face, and the more we are pressured simply to fill the job, the more important it is to look carefully at our manager-building policies and skills and to take a fresh, creative approach.

## WHAT MAKES A GOOD SERVICE MANAGER?

The dictionary gives this definition of "manage":

> To control, guide. To have charge of; to direct, conduct, administer. To get others to do what one wishes, especially by skill, tact, or flattery. To accomplish results by skill.

Selecting a good manager requires thought and ingenuity. But each of you has a different meaning for the word "manager," and regards "manager" in the light of the specific business you're in. Then there is the kind of manager to be thought of. Is he or she a sales manager? A technical manager? In addition, the kind of field service you're involved in must be examined. In one company, service might be only assistance to the sales department. In another company, it might be product service or warranty service. And in yet another, service is a profit center and not only performs service but sells it as a product.

For each of you, the responsibility you assign to a field manager may be different. Is he responsible for people who report directly to him? How about material? Does he have a budget for cost? Is he responsible for making a profit? Is he involved in forecasting and planning, or does that come from the home office? How about sales? What's he the manager of: A branch office? A dealership? A distributorship or a subsidiary?

In determining the specific knowledge needed to manage a business in the field, each or us has a different set of qualifications, but there are some things common to all of us in how we look at field management. Whatever the combination of products and services in your business, the field manager needs the capability of running that business. The chances are pretty good that you don't want him to be only a salesman or a technician, or only one thing. What we really need to run our business around the country is a *businessman.* Of course he has to understand the nuts and bolts of running a particular business that is somehow different from any other. Yes, he must be familiar with the technicalities of the equipment he's servicing. But above all, he must be a businessman.

He's responsible for running the business, so he has to understand it. Whatever the form of your field organization, the manager comes into contact with customers, so he's a salesman. And he has to deal with the people who work in his office, so he's an administrator. Whatever your financial structure, he's responsible for cost or profit or both, and probably has some connection with the growth of the business.

Almost anyone good enough to be selected by you for field management has enough ambition and self-esteem to try to better himself, so he will try on his own to learn more about the business. The chances are good that whatever he does to try to improve himself will be within the same area of endeavor in which he was expert in the first place. So our responsibility is to direct him on the proper path: We have to take a specialist and make him into a businessman. That means we have to teach him those skills and show him how to get the most out of them.

## WHERE DO WE FIND GOOD SERVICE MANAGERS?

When we start looking for a manager for a field operation, the chances are good that we will promote someone within the company and preferably within the service department itself. In addition to getting someone with experience in our business, this makes it plain to the rest of the people in the service department that promotion is possible and that they do have some place to go.

There's always the chance that you can promote someone already in management from a small office to a larger one. If this works out, it will make the selection easier. If this type of backup is not available, look through the whole service department. Don't limit yourself to the areas that are normally considered the development grounds for management (that is, sales and marketing); look in the technical areas—the engineers or the service people—and look in the administrative area—the dispatchers or the people who have been running your warranty control system. And of course, if you have sales and marketing capability within your service department, look there.

People in sales and marketing will normally be more visible because of their natural aggressiveness, but don't forget those other areas. You may very well have some outstanding people with a lot of potential in other parts of your company who just do not have much visibility at the moment.

Look in the smaller offices. Don't forget that because of their broader responsibilities people in smaller offices have a tendency to learn about your operation more quickly than people who work in large offices and who have more narrowly defined jobs. People in service tend to become rather parochial, but don't ignore potentially outstanding people in the other organizations within your division. And don't forget the other divisions, either. Good people are working there, too, and it could pay off for you to find out who they are and to let them know you're looking.

Look outside the company, too. Your competitors may have some outstanding people you'd like to have on your payroll. It might also be worth giving some attention to related service industries because you are seeking someone with the potential of becoming a manager, not just a person who knows the nuts and bolts of your specific equipment. And if you happen to run across someone in a nonrelated industry whose management potential or actual managerial performance impresses you, remember that management skills are more important than specific technical knowledge. When you're sure you've found a good manager, take him—no matter where he's from.

## HOW ARE GOOD SERVICE MANAGERS SELECTED?

The selection process is one of the most important factors in building managers. Look back on how you've done this in the past when you needed a manager. In selecting them, did you choose them for their management potential or as a reward for their past performance?

There are many different ways for people to win promotions. Here are nine of them.

1. *Outstanding sales performance.* Although it's rarely the factor considered, it has clout. Yet many disillusioned general managers will affirm that top salespeople don't necessarily make top managers.

2. *The right time . . . the right place.* Lady Luck

is kind to the people who work the "cupcake" territories that contain big, healthy accounts. Processions of home office brass are constantly making pilgrimages to these areas, and the local manager serves as their escort, thereby providing an additional opportunity for visibility!

3. *Influential sponsorship.* When a manager takes someone under his wing, the chances of that person's getting promoted are related directly to the manager's influence in the company. If the manager has been successful and controls an important district, his recommendation is important. And if the person being sponsored has a forceful personality and friends in the home office, his or her future is assured.

4. *An extraordinary single achievement.* Sometimes a blockbuster sale or victory in a contest or some other all-out single effort will catapult someone into prominence. From then on, past failings are overlooked and that person can do no wrong. If a managerial opening occurs while his or her accomplishment is still fresh in people's minds, a promotion is assured.

5. *Political know-how.* Some are expert at campaigning for themselves—they spend more time at self-promotion than they do working. They deftly manipulate and attempt to accumulate votes. In a real sense, they are candidates for promotion and it's important to find out if they have capabilities other than self-promotion.

6. *Winning personality.* The "personality people" charm everyone they come in contact with: customers, peers, supervisors, and home office staff. They're well liked by everyone. But if they become managers and fail, it's a bewildering and unhappy event. The general feeling is, how could this have happened to such a nice person?

7. *Promotion by default.* The one who goes about business conscientiously and performs reasonably well, follows instructions to the letter, and doesn't antagonize anyone sometimes wins promotion by default. Generally, when a particularly unpopular candidate is being touted for a vacancy, the steady, undistinguished person is hastily called upon to fill the opening. This blocks the way for the hard-to-handle candidate who may have a better record.

8. *Formal screening procedures.* With the aid of a company psychologist or outside consultant, some companies assemble a battery of tests to measure intelligence, interest patterns, and personality traits. In other companies, candidates for management positions are challenged with a series of tests, interviews, and performance simulations that seem to have been developed by the CIA.

Methods such as these have their advantages: measuring certain characteristics scientifically, eliminating some of the guesswork, removing some of the subjective, emotional bases for decision-making. But there are still judgments to be made. The computer cannot identify the candidate who possesses management potential unless it has been told what to look for. For the results of these techniques to be meaningful, variables on which decisions are based must have been meticulously correlated with objective performance criteria rather than going by someone's ill-founded theory that "dominant, extroverted men with a good sense of humor make the best managers." And without thorough analysis, these procedures often make incorrect predictions about women and members of minority groups (which is, incidentally, a violation of EEOC guidelines).

9. *Encouragement and development by interested*

*supervisors.* Those who are intelligent, who want to be managers, and have successful mentors to model themselves after are destined for eventual promotion —perhaps not in their present companies, but certainly somewhere. With proper encouragement and systematic development, such people will grow into effective managers.

But considering the pressure on you to select a candidate for that immediate opening, and since you (like the rest of us) probably don't have at hand a carefully chosen list of candidates, you may have looked for people who were doing well in their present assignments. And chances are that you limited your field of choice to someone local to save the cost of a transfer—or you may have been forced to.

In a sense, you gave someone a reward for past performance, but there's a problem here waiting to show itself at the worst time. An outstanding salesperson may have no real interest in running a business. The best technician may have a mortal fear of talking to people, and may also suffer from the conversion from worker to supervisor. Some people fail as managers because they just can't force themselves to put down the screwdriver or the briefcase. And if you're moving in a manager from another area of expertise, you may have someone trying to run a field operation on the basis of ideas from a half-remembered college marketing course.

Therefore, promotion as a method of rewarding performance has drawbacks as well as advantages. Let's face it, rewards for performance are present in every facet of our lives, and they can be useful in reinforcing desired behavior. They just shouldn't be the only basis for management selection.

## HOW TO SPOT A POTENTIALLY GOOD SERVICE MANAGER

We often have personal preferences about who is promotable. Have you ever heard statements like these?

□ Appearance is important. I like a man who's tall, conservative in dress, and has a bearing of self-confidence. A little gray hair helps.

□ The people I promote are always well liked by other members of the group. They're highly social and have a sense of humor.

□ Loyalty is something I look for. If a man hasn't been behind me 100%, I feel he won't be loyal to the company or anyone he supervises.

As long as we search for people with superpersonalities, measure applicants by "gut" feelings, and select people with backgrounds similar to ours (played football, went to our alma mater, served in the Navy), we will make a lot of costly mistakes.

In every group there's a natural leader. The one who leads the discussion in meetings, the one who always makes the presentation speech at parties, the spokesperson—they're all demonstrating that they want to lead. Those who have performed well have more visibility. You'll know they're there and they will automatically form part of the population from which you'll make a selection. That's their reward—to be *considered*. From here on, though, the selection has to be based on *potential*.

What is the candidate's potential for management? If one has made your selection list, we can assume he has the required intelligence, but for a manager you need a person who can use intelligence. Assuming that you have explained what management means to you and your company, the candidate must want to be a manager and must want to make that commitment.

Somewhere along the line they have to take a hard look at themselves, and you may have to see that this happens during part of the interviewing sequence. Why do they want to be managers? Some answers could be power, money, autonomy, achievement, or recognition. Are they willing to pay the price? They'll have to spend more time away from home. There will be personal risk, because instead of harming a single small area, their mistakes can hurt the entire department. Since all the help you and others give along the way won't count for much unless they want to improve, do they have the will for self-development?

To be truly effective, managers must have not only the creativity to allow the development of new ideas, but also the initiative to present those ideas. They must also have the guts to fight for them now and then. When they have fought and lost, they must have the fortitude to accept the refusal and keep on trying. They must have the ability to walk the fine line between fighting for the branch, the office, or the distributorship, and doing what may be best for the company as a whole.

They must be able to look ahead and understand the effects of the future on the business. You can't run an effective business without the ability to plan and forecast. This means that changes and their effects cannot be discredited just because they don't fit into the preconceived mold of yesterday and today.

So it's quite a problem selecting a manager—at least if you consider all these factors. It may even seem that you can't afford to spend that much time on it, but on the other hand, can you afford to spend less time? Can you afford managers who have to be replaced every two or three years? Remember, it's not only the bother of it all, it's the fact that your business didn't do what it was supposed to do for those years. It didn't grow, or it lost money, or some of your customers got mad and left.

If you're part of a large corporation and your personnel department has developed a way to help you evaluate these points, that's fine. But it remains your responsibility as a manager to select the people who have the best chance of success and to develop good management. It's doubtful that anyone could meet all of these admittedly very difficult criteria at the start, since that will require training and experience. If we can agree, however, that the initial selection is of prime importance, then we must invest the necessary time and effort to choose the candidate with the highest potential.

# 7

# Building a field manager: Training

THE WAY it usually all starts is that we select the management candidate and make an offer. To people being offered their first chance at management, the glory of it all may temporarily outweigh their inclination to ask searching questions. Our discussion emphasizes the challenge, the opportunity (both only in general terms), and the fact that we need a decision right away. So, overwhelmed by our obvious high opinion of their past efforts and perhaps having visions of future vice-presidencies, they take the big step.

So we give them the job. Probably the reason we needed a manager in the first place was that the operation was a complete mess. During the first month, they're buried in paperwork they don't understand, but they can't do too much about that because they're spending about 12 hours a day trying to straighten things out.

By a painful process of trial and error, they start learning what is expected of a supervisor. They must learn to work within the organization, be sensitive to the expectations of superiors, and be able to negotiate with peers. They must learn to plan, budget, schedule, analyze work flow, and constantly increase productivity. They must respond to requests, demands, and needs, and be concerned with output. Most important, they must learn how to understand subordinates and work with them effectively. This involves a variety of interpersonal skills, including the ability to stimulate, persuade, satisfy, prod, accommodate, reassure, advise, and motivate. They must make sure that the people under their supervision understand their jobs and the quantity of work they are expected to produce. They must help their subordinates perform that job well, and recognize and correct mistakes. They must teach their subordinates how to moderate conflict, settle grievances, listen carefully, make decisions, solve problems, control, delegate, appraise, train, and speak and write clearly.

To help new managers learn all this, we may send them to a seminar during their first year, but only for a day or so because of the high cost of hotels and travel. During the first year they may even get a visit or two from a regional or home office manager, but these are short and usually oriented toward specific and immediate problems.

But soon they make a few poor decisions, and we notice that the business is not progressing as we think it should be. We have a talk with them, possibly saying "we had hopes for you, we had faith in your ability to do a better job, but you're not delivering the results. You'd better shape up and turn this operation around." Now in a state of panic, they make more bad decisions and things get worse. In the meantime, of course, several bosses visit to tell them they're in trouble (as if they didn't know), and after another year we get rid of them. In doing so we tell them what their errors were, and after the shock wears off, they probably wonder why we didn't say something about the errors two years earlier. This pattern sounds familiar: We've probably all seen this play acted out a few times by real people.

Whose fault was the failure? Certainly not theirs: From their very first day on the job they had some very specific needs that weren't answered, and we did not provide them with the tools necessary to do the job. They were programmed for failure. Would we even dream of sending a service person on the road with a broken screwdriver and a burned out meter? Of course not, but all too often we send a manager out to hunt tigers with a BB gun, and when the tiger eats him we shake our heads resignedly and buy another box of BBs for his successor.

## THE NEEDS OF NEW MANAGERS

We may have to forget about our needs for a while and consider the needs of the new managers. Remember, the odds are good that if we satisfy their needs, they'll take care of ours. To start with, if we select people properly, they will have all the potential they can use; what they need is tools to work with. The best way to start is to explain to them the company philosophy or what our purpose is. Perhaps we're striving to keep the new product working long enough to get through the warranty period. We may be subsidizing new offices to get them started. Our aim may be growth of business at the expense of profit until a certain level is attained. Perhaps our purpose is growth with a certain level of profit maintained. Maybe we are trying to provide warranty and ongoing product service at zero profit (or no loss) or to provide these services within a specific cost budget.

The point is that to be effective, new managers must know what our real goals and aims are. They have to know what is expected, and we cannot assume they will know this without our making the information available. After all, these few instructions will be the basis on which they will build their whole management technique. In any company there are some specific things that a manager needs to know to run the business. One example of these would be financial and accounting information. Each company has its own financial structure and accounting techniques, and a lot of reports. New managers must know how this is structured, what it means, and how it works. They must understand which parts of the reporting system they can have an effect on and the ones over which they have no control. (For example, they may have full control of labor costs and very little control of certain overheads.) The point, however, is that to be effective, they cannot be left to learn this through on-the-job experience.

If an effort is not made to teach new managers these financial and accounting techniques and to give them an understanding of the reporting systems, they will learn over a period of time how the system works. Actually they'll *think* they know how it works, but because they will have based some of their understanding on misconceptions, they will surely be led into making some poor business decisions.

In every financial reporting system there are things that don't work exactly the way we would like them to. Two lines on a statement do not add up properly unless a manual adjustment is made each month by the accounting department—a line reporting material cost that for some reason known only to the data processing group also includes some labor. Perhaps you report labor cost through the twentieth of the month and material through the tenth of the next month. Managers have to understand these things to understand the business. If they are not told how they work, they will make poor judgments on the basis of the financial information given to them, or will spend an inordinate amount of time trying to understand the reports and how they are really put together. All managers should understand the financial reporting and accounting systems, but particularly new managers who are most likely to be in the position of knowing nothing about this side of the business when they step into their jobs, and must therefore be protected from their ignorance. The only way to be sure that they have the right information is for us to make sure that we give it to them—and in a format that they can use.

New managers also have informational needs in the administrative area including all personnel matters such as hiring, firing, raises, promotions, and salary administration. They need the most up-to-date copies of any procedures that your company may have. In the most important areas where policy is involved, they need instruction and training in addition to any available manuals. Do they know how to handle employee relations in a positive manner? Just because a person has that wondrous thing called "potential," you cannot assume this specific capability. Knowing how to get along with their people is also essential.

The manager's relationship with peers is also most important. New managers may have a certain amount of reluctance to participate in conversations and dis-

cussions at meetings. Therefore it is most important
for them to be given the opportunity to attend as many
meetings as possible with other service managers. This
will not only make them feel at home with the group
but will give them a good opportunity to learn. It will
also help them begin to think of themselves as really
being a part of management.

Another important part in the administrative area is
clerical functions. How is paperwork handled? Who
collects and prepares report information to go to regional, district, or home offices? When are the reports
due? How is the information developed? How is it
transmitted? In what kind of format? What training is
available for clerical people? In the technical area,
whatever information is required by the service person
must be available, along with information on training,
instruments, tools, and whatever policies and procedures have been established with regard to performance of service.

In the area of sales they need to know what sales of
company products or services they might be responsible
for. How are quotas assigned? What pricing policies
are established? If salespeople are part of the organization, how are they trained? If they are paid motivational money such as incentive or commission, how
is this calculated and controlled?

Another area of prime importance to the new manager is the management of time. Without specific training in this area, there will surely be a tendency to spend
the majority of one's available time on detail work that
can best be done by others. There are several excellent
books, manuals, and training seminars to help alleviate
this problem, and new managers should be encouraged
to make use of them.

We must remember the effects of this new job on

the newly appointed manager. Initially there will be a certain amount of apprehension and the fear of not doing well or of making mistakes. Most new managers will initially have considerable difficulty in letting go of old habits, and they will have a natural tendency to continue performing their previous tasks (with which they are more comfortable). A worker gets satisfaction from short-term accomplishments; a manager, from progress toward long-term goals. The new manager needs assistance from us in helping to get through this initial period of apprehension and worry, and also needs direction and help in learning to delegate the proper tasks to others in the organization.

They must also be made to realize that they will always be responsible for things over which they have no authority. They must manage people they don't hire, sell things whose quality they don't control, and implement procedures that they did not initiate. That's the way life really is: responsibility is always greater than authority.

Try to remember back to when you first became a manager and the fears you had—the fears of not producing what you thought your management expected of you, the fear of being involved in a job you didn't know too much about, and the loneliness that resulted from all of your friends and former associates' expecting direction from you. These same people had spent time with you discussing the endless reorganization of the company, and you'd all laughed together over how to get Friday afternoon off and how to squeeze an extra three dollars out of the expense account. New managers will eventually learn to handle these things, but if they are to do it in a reasonable amount of time they will need help. There is also the matter of the relationship of the new manager to other units of the company. One thing that may be of considerable importance in some companies is interdepartmental rivalry, and a new manager should be given a feeling for how this should be handled. If carried too far, this rivalry can of course have a negative effect: esprit de corps within a department or office can be most beneficial. As long as the members of the group feel superior to other groups within the company, they will have a tendency to act superior, too.

The manager should be aware of the policy and procedures used by the company in developing budgets. In any organization, there will be a certain amount of competition between various groups for budget money. Since the service manager will be responsible for developing the budget, this can probably be done better with an understanding of how the games are played within the organization.

## HOW TO MEET THE NEEDS OF NEW MANAGERS

The first and most important thing to do is to be fair, honest, and above all, open. Make them aware of what is expected—they need to know the objectives. Since there is a wealth of information available on MBO and how to administer such a program, we needn't go into detail about it. But we should clearly define managers' personal objectives and put them in writing. They should have a copy of their job description, and if such a document is not available it should be prepared. Then we should go over it with them word by word so they can have no possible misunderstanding of their duties and responsibilities. In addition to learning the direction of the business as a whole, they should be given a full understanding of the departmental goals, and of how those goals affect them.

Perhaps the most basic step in answering new managers' needs is communicating with them about some of the matters we don't usually talk about. Talk about the fears you know they have, about their relationship with others, about how to relate to their people, how to develop an esprit de corps, and how to improve their image with their peers and superiors. Many times a manager's deficiencies in these areas are the things we as their superiors discuss among ourselves—and judge them on. But we don't talk about it to them, possibly because we feel that these matters are too personal, or are the sort of thing they have to do alone. They probably *can* do it alone, but it may take longer—or it may not happen at all.

## THE IMPORTANCE OF MOTIVATION

One thing they really need is motivation—that inner feeling that makes a person want to do something. This can be obscured, however, by fears and frustrations. Since new managers are very justifiably concerned about the new job and what the boss will think of them, they may very well not be able to produce unless they are motivated. There are as many books on motivation as there are ways to motivate people, so this discussion will be as brief and as basic as possible.

### Money as a motivator

Although money in itself is not a motivator, and doesn't alone create that inner feeling, the lack of money is one of the best de-motivators available. Despite the many theories to the contrary, there are very few people who do not need or want more money. Examine your own feelings. Of course, you're worth more than you're getting. We all are, and everybody understands that. And we each know (or hope) in our hearts that there is a job out there for someone with our exact capabilities, and at a salary twice as high as our current one! In the real world, we don't really expect to have our salary doubled, but if we are really underpaid and are aware of it, chances are that we won't ever get those feelings of being motivated.

Regardless of written policies, pay for performance standards, and the other things that companies say, there are two real-life facts you can depend on: first, it's harder to get a large in-grade raise approved than to get a salary increase on promotion; and second, if you ever let yourself get behind on a person's salary, you'll have a difficult time catching up. So the secret is that when you promote people, give them enough of a raise to put them where they should be. Decide what the job is worth, and offer them at least that much, maybe a bit more. Don't try to buy them cheaply to save $40 a month. That's not economy; that's dumb!

### The "little" things

There are some things we can do that will motivate but that won't cost all that much, and most of us won't admit we even want them. One example of this is a better office—carpeting, windows, drapes, a nice desk, a good chair, perhaps a colored phone. When they travel, let them go first class. Let them carry a decent attache case. Don't argue about the cost of taking a taxi. Surely you have to maintain management control of expenses, but if you can trust managers with your field office, you can trust their judgment on expenses. That doesn't mean you give them a free hand—just don't question them unless something is obviously wrong. Treat them like the high-caliber executives you want them to be.

Then there's their status with peers, which you can easily improve. Call on them at meetings. Ask them to speak about the best part of their operation. Be sure to introduce them to other managers (especially senior managers). When there's a discussion, ask for their opinions, and get them involved. Make them feel important!

In other words, concentrate on the little rewards as much as the big ones, and make them frequent. The job they have now requires day-to-day, hour-to-hour effort and perseverance. Their prizes, however, may be in the distant future. Successful managers develop their own systems of internal rewards and orientation to long-term goals, but you must give them frequent pats on the back, especially at the start.

It's really a matter of different strokes for different folks. Some people want money. Others like money, but will work harder for recognition. Still others will really turn on when you challenge them with a task. "We've tried to do this for years, but nobody could make it work. Maybe it's just impossible." What you have to do in each case is to find out which button to push.

### How to de-motivate people

There are also ways to turn people off almost automatically:

1. Set goals that are unattainable, so the person feels at once that success is impossible.
2. Fail to recognize accomplishments.
3. Make demands without providing enough training to meet them. This makes people feel incompetent.

4. Don't provide a long-range plan or guidelines for their behavior.
5. Make programs so complex that they're difficult to understand. Or have so many things going on at once that it's difficult for a field employee to identify with any one program long enough to get excited.

De-motivators are one of the main reasons for failure in field management. A staff person can provide motivational tools and opportunities for people in the field, but can also provide de-motivators by putting roadblocks in the way. Asking for too many reports and making paperwork too difficult is a good example. In general, motivation comes from above in an organization. *You* must plan to be the motivator: if you don't, nobody will. Simplicity is the key. The person being motivated must know what to do, when to do it, and how to do it. Esprit de corps is important, and people who have such feelings tend to be motivated more easily than those who have no interest in their own group.

### Some ways to improve managers' motivation

To conclude this discussion of motivation, here are several ways to improve the motivation of your managers.

1. Make motivation programs clear, concise, and understandable to all.
2. Understand that the major responsibility of staff people is to motivate line management.
3. Be sure that we consider the motivation or de-motivation of people in every program we develop.
4. Show a genuine interest in your managers.
5. Don't ever hold a person back from a promotion because he or she is valuable to you.

6. When credit is due for accomplishments, spread it around. Give all the people involved credit for the part they played.


## TRAINING THE NEW MANAGER

We have been talking about the needs of the new field manager and how to serve those needs. That means that we have to teach him how to do the things he has to do —and that's training. Training, as applied to field management, is perhaps our greatest challenge. But before considering this problem, let's digress for a moment. Ask yourself these questions:

1. Do you have a procedure that some of your field offices don't or won't use?
2. Is there a new program of some kind that some of them won't use until the others prove it works?
3. Have you ever had the feeling that a few of your managers don't understand the situation?

If your answer to any or all of these questions was yes, you've got the same problem as all the rest of us. You can always call it a communications problem, meaning that you didn't say it right, or they didn't hear it right, or both.

We've all had the experience of announcing a new policy or procedure to the field. We put it in an official bulletin, we refer to it in several letters, repeat it in the company newsletter, and talk about it at meetings. But even after we fire two people for not paying attention, there are still several managers making statements such as: "It doesn't apply to me; it's for the others," or "It's a dumb policy, so I won't do it," or "I'll have to remember to start doing that," or "I haven't had time," or "We have a very special problem in this office, unlike any other, and . . ."

You communicated several times, and they heard it several times, but it was ineffective. My point is, you probably needed to train them. You needed to give them the reason for doing what you wanted them to do: Why should I? How do I? Who does it? When do we start? What are the benefits to me?

There are several ways to train people, the most obvious being a classroom in which you talk and they listen. Then there's the seminar, which resembles the classroom, except that there is talk in both directions. The students get involved, and you all learn from each other. And think about including workshops, too—hands-on practice in actually doing whatever it is you want them to do. Programmed courses will do the job for a large part of your needs. You can use tapes, slides, filmstrips, manuals, any medium that fits the subject matter. There's no travel cost, and the course can be gone over as many times as the student desires.

On-the-job training is always good, but it has to be understood that this doesn't mean the "college of hard knocks." It means instead that the manager's manager has to invest some time in the process. Managers need someone to listen to their problems, and to walk them through the solutions; someone who has already made the mistakes to tell them what to avoid; someone to explain the things that seemed so simple at the seminar last month, but just don't seem to work in the office. So what we're really saying is that they need to be led. That means leadership—from you.

There are differences to consider in training a new manager as opposed to one with experience. The new ones have very special needs because they're at ground zero, and it's up to you to decide what they should get first. About the best place to start is with basics: what the job is, your philosophy of management, department goals and objectives, and what's expected. After you completely cover this basic knowledge they should have of their job and what it is, it's time to start on what to do and how to do it. This includes things like financial statements and reports, interviewing and hiring, personnel policies, administration, goal setting and MBO, forecasting and planning, coaching and training of personnel, cost control, and union negotiations. For your company, some of these may not be applicable, or you may be able to think of others that apply better to your specific case. The point is that the initial course or group of courses should be about the things that they'll be doing, and that they'll need the most help with.

A most important point is that the training must be in absorbable pieces. It's better to have ten separate courses, each on a specific subject, than one large course on "how to be a manager." It also helps if the information is in sequence. Chances are that people will understand it better in small doses, and in about the same order in which problems are likely to arise in their new jobs. Imagine the effect if, just as the monthly statements arrive in the mail, the new managers got a filmstrip and tape cassette explaining how to use and understand those particular statements.

This kind of training costs money to produce, but you have to consider what it does for you. With it you can get specific material to the manager when it's needed most, and when he is most receptive. Also it can be used over and over again.

This brings up the refresher course. Training new managers is a constant process, particularly in a growing organization. There's another need that we should always remember: the new manager never finishes training. Not only that, they're only new managers (for training purposes) until the day after the first training session. Just about the time they get through all the courses you've got, the world changes and it's time to start over. Since doing this is the only way to keep things going, and the benefits are so outstanding, we should really look at it as an opportunity rather than as a difficulty.

Training is also necessary for those who work for the manager. Although they may be on a different level, these people have the same continuing needs, and the manager will need help to meet them. We're talking about training them to train others, which does not mean that they must absorb every bit of information needed. However, they must be able to see that the training gets done.

Since the subject matter of this training will be more technical in nature, it needs to be packaged—one subject at a time, and perhaps only part of a subject. If you are covering the service of a particular piece of equipment, you may do better with individual packages on theory, operations, or troubleshooting and repair. The proper breakdown will vary with the subject and therefore must be decided each time. The packages should be complete with slides, manuals, and quiz sheets so they can be used in the field without excess effort. Organize the courses in proper sequence. For instance, if you're talking about combustion control systems, make the first course basic—what combustion is, how flames work and so on. Next might be simple control systems, then the more sophisticated, then troubleshooting. Graduate from basic theory to complex systems.

When you consider all the training needs of the new manager, and that they should be met within a specific time period, it would be very difficult if not impossible to remember them all without a list. This will give you a more formal way to remind yourself of what is to be discussed each time you meet. Although the detailed items on a list will vary for each company, and perhaps for each manager, here are some general headings you might consider.

1. *Overview.* Discussion of history, condition of the office, trends, performances, customers, existing problems, and management attitudes of predecessors.
2. *Management philosophy.* Where you've been, where you're going, and how you plan to get there.
3. *Finance.* Profit and loss, costs, budgets, plans, and forecasts.
4. *Territory.* Where employees and customers are located. Travel time and customer coverage.
5. *Manpower.* Capabilities, potential, performance, future needs, and specific problems.
6. *Training.* Plans for the manager and employees.
7. *Obligations.* Reports, projects, meetings, special problems.
8. *Responsibility.* The manager's responsibilities and authority; reporting chains.

When this list is tailored to meet your specific needs, it will become a valuable tool to ensure that the new manager gets the help needed, particularly if you list the items in priority order and include dates. This will help new managers make it through the first 120 days with less difficulty. Chances for success are much greater when people are given a better level of organized support during this critical period.

Another basic point: many of the more important things you try to communicate to your field managers (new programs or better use of existing programs, for example) can't be delegated to someone else or covered in a brief conversation. Take the time to do them right, and do it yourself. Here are some specific suggestions:

- Have a meeting rather than telling them one on one. When compared with the results, the travel cost is really insignificant.
- Hold the meetings in a pleasant place. Although there will frequently be feelings that meetings in Florida, Jamaica, or the Bahamas in February are a boondoggle, they aren't. They're more effective, and they really don't cost that much more.
- Spend some time and money putting together a good script and good visuals with impact. Use music, flags, bells, funny hats—anything you can to get *impact*. Use your imagination! And have fun!
- Make your meetings the kind that people look forward to.

This is really training in its highest form. You're not only involving new managers in the subject matter of the meeting, you're also teaching them to conduct effective meetings themselves.

One of the best possible ways to train managers to be effective, and to be the businesspeople you want them to be, is to involve them in planning. There's no way to go through a planning program without getting to understand the business as a whole, and that it is many separate pieces all fitting together. Sales, billings, costs, manpower, facilities, expansion, training, new markets—it's all in there.

Finally, it's important to let new managers make mistakes, because we all do. Be sure they know that although you expect a good ratio of successes to failures, people will not be fired for making mistakes.

### McCAFFERTY'S LAW NUMBER SEVEN
#### It's better to try something and fail, than to do nothing and succeed.

## EVALUATING NEW MANAGERS' PERFORMANCE

How do you evaluate a manager? Objectively, using numbers and specific yardsticks such as sales, cost, profit, and warranty claims? Or subjectively, considering feelings, personal analysis, and so on? Probably both. Neither is really complete without the other.

On the basis of how your particular business is put together, there are always numbers you can use. Whatever it is you do, there's a way to measure how much of it got done, when it got done, or how well. Numerical evaluation does give objectivity, and leaves less room for emotion, and that's the reason that at least a part of the evaluation must be of this kind.

But subjective evaluation is also necessary. A manager's attitude is a determinate thing, even though it can't be assigned a number. Are their customers happy? How do they handle their people? Do they prepare them for advancement? Do they prepare themselves for advancement? Perhaps they do an outstanding job of working within the system and of suggesting improvements, rather than going off in a different direction. Consider how they handle meetings, and how they come across with management.

Earlier we spoke about giving the new managers written objectives and about telling them what's expected from them. If you are going to evaluate how well people are doing their jobs—and thereby affect their future—it's only fair to let them know what you're going to measure them on. And after you do the evaluation, you should make them aware of the results.

If they're doing well, say so. If they need to improve in certain areas, say so. It's important that they get feedback, and the secret is in giving it to them regularly. An appraisal should be informal and brief, and should be performed separately from salary administration. Focus on their performance rather than criticizing them personally. Remember, the only response to a personal attack is defensiveness or a personal counterattack. The object is to have them leave the appraisal session thinking about how they can go about strengthening their performance, not licking their wounds.

New managers fail because they fall short of what their supervisors expect. However, these expectations usually aren't precisely spelled out or agreed to in advance by both manager and supervisor. Sometimes, new managers may feel that their performance is exceptional, whereas you may believe just the opposite. Often a manager may be failing and neither of you may realize it until well after the fact. That's because failure is usually silent: bells don't ring, lights don't flash, and skyrockets don't go off.

Because undetected failures can be extraordinarily costly, it's vital that new managers and their supervisors understand the causes of failure. These can be divided into two broad categories: assisted failures, in which the new manager is led or pushed into failure; and self-failures. It's our responsibility to observe these in their infancy—and do something to prevent them from getting out of control.

After all our other work in building a manager is done, what lets us measure whether or not it was effective is our evaluation. That's where the results come in, and that's how we can decide how effective we are as managers. And it's where we have the opportunity to correct our mistakes.

## CONCLUSIONS

The managers of this generation face an unprecedented challenge. They are the first generation whose formal education and training threaten to become obsolete before they can fully exploit it. A symptom of this obsolescence is a feeling of time pressure—the demands of the job can no longer be met in the time available by using the old methods.

To live up to this challenge will be quite an accomplishment, and it will take a special kind of person. Leadership requires courage, boldness, and a willingness to accept risk. Leadership involves insecurity: individuality, of course, cannot run rampant over the larger purpose of the organization. It is the successful accomplishment of an individual task, rather than the techniques used to approach it, that should be the criterion for evaluating its merit. Responsibility, authority, and the right to individual work method must go hand in hand.

In American industry and business we need courage, not complacency; leadership, not conformity. To provide the leadership and courage to meet these needs, the demand will be great for the change seeker who is a person with a mission that overshadows personal ambition. These people must have the intellectual and physical courage and originality to pursue a personal vision despite all accidents and obstacles, and must have vision and goals so lofty that they know they will fall short of them. This knowledge will give them the all-important trait of humility.

Although this may sound a bit farfetched, think about it for a moment: don't you have a big dream project—one of those that takes years to accomplish—

that you've been working on? Words like "mission," "vision," and "lofty" may seem rather profound, but of all the managers we build, the odds are that the ones who are most successful over the years will be people with missions.

Good managers have certain skills and attitudes that make them good at managing. It's our job to make it possible for them to develop these skills and attitudes. And it's their responsibility to use the tools we give them. We can supply the tools and the motivation, but not the action.

And remember that there is nothing wrong in managers' enjoying their work, liking their fellow workers, or feeling that what they do in their job in some way serves mankind. And they *do* serve mankind: serving customers is an honorable pursuit; maximizing profit to promote growth and create more jobs is an honorable pursuit; and the constant compromise and cooperation between them, their friends, their fellow employees, and their customers is an honorable pursuit.

Being a manager is no longer—or at least should no longer be—a reward for longevity or performance in another field. It's a specialty, one that deserves our attention and our respect. If within your organization you're responsible for building managers, that responsibility must be taken seriously. There's no easy way to handle it. If we are to do this job right, it will take time and hard work. None of the steps necessary to build a manager will happen by themselves.

Remember, the people who in 15 years will be the national service managers, the vice-presidents, the general managers, and the regional heads will probably come from the ranks of the new managers you start building this year. Always remember that you're not just filling a vacancy; you're helping to decide the future of your company.

And there's another point to consider:

## McCAFFERTY'S LAW NUMBER EIGHT
**Always hire people smarter than yourself.**

Now we know what can be accomplished, or to put it another way, we have recognized the problem—and a problem recognized is half solved. With time and effort, we can build field managers—good field managers. But to be realistic, why should we? After all, it's a lot of hard work and we're busy.

For starters, good field managers help the business run better, and help make the profits higher, the costs lower, and the problems fewer. These kinds of changes have to be reflected in your salary, your image, and your reputation. You'll be helping to develop the future management team for your company, and the development of this all-important resource will reflect favorably on you. And there's a personal payoff: whenever you help any person get closer to operating at his or her full potential, you get a good feeling and a real sense of accomplishment.

The better you are at building managers, the more of it you'll have to do, because your business will grow, and you'll need more of them. The word will get around that you develop good people, and you'll probably lose a few of them. But in working at building managers, you're bettering your future and everyone else's.

# 8

# Developing an effective field force

A SERVICE BUSINESS is unique in that its only real asset is its people and their skills. A manufacturer, or the manufacturing part of your company, will have a large asset base in buildings, tooling, and machinery. A company in transportation will have trucks, trains, or aircraft. A service business can very easily lease its buildings or its vehicles and rent much of the rest of what it uses. Its assets will be the people, the tools they use, and their knowledge and skills, most of which will never appear on a balance sheet. This is the reason the ROA in a service business is so interesting.

Although people and their skills are quite difficult to separate, let's talk about the people first. What is a field person? Is he or she a service person, a field engineer, or a factory representative? To make up an effective field force there must be sales, technical, administrative, and supervisory people. At this point I will not go into the development and training of an effective field sales force, which is another subject altogether, but will instead concentrate more on the operational field force, the people who perform the services sold. A point must be made here, however: the sales and operations parts of your business must be coordinated, must understand each other, must work together, must each be as dedicated and as professional as the other.

## McCAFFERTY'S LAW NUMBER NINE
### The services you provide must be performed in a highly professional manner.

"Each as professional as the other" is stated that way for a reason: in many companies the salespeople are considered to be the professionals, whereas operations people are thought to be the "greasy-fingered" people in the back room. When operations people are encouraged to shape up, it is often along the lines of, "Why can't you be as professional as the salespeople are?" Were you ever asked why you didn't get A's in arithmetic like Johnny or why you couldn't be polite like Arthur? If you were, you can surely remember that those early motivational efforts failed. It is wrong to think of needing to upgrade the operations people to someone else's level, but you should expect them to maintain the highest possible level of performance in their own terms.

You may be assured that, given the proper motivation, the technical people you hire will be as highly professional in the performance of their responsibilities and as proud of that performance as anyone could possibly be. Although this is perhaps an oversimplification, the only real difference between a field service person and anyone else is that he likes to be in the field, likes the association with equipment and systems, and likes to work with his hands. His preference for the specific work functions he performs each day as a part of his job are somewhat different and that is the only difference. In all other respects his needs and wants, likes and dislikes, are the same as everyone else's.

Their problems, however, seem to be common to every company in the service business. Look at the situation from the service person's point of view. There is competition in the service business, and it's hard to sell service contracts. There are hundreds of reasons it's hard to make money—inflation, the economy, and so on. When material is ordered, it never seems to get delivered on time. Some of the customers seem to expect things that neither service people nor the equipment can possibly do. Service people account for that by accusing salespeople of raising impossible expectations in the customers; salespeople attribute it to the service people's lack of competence. We've got problems because, from a branch viewpoint, the regional managers don't know what it's like in the real world, and the home office people are so far away from the business that they have no sense of the day-to-day problems involved. The people in the factory don't understand the real needs of the business, and it's obvious to the factory people that *nobody* understands them. The service reports that have to be filled out are too complicated, and many of the parts necessary for proper service may not be available. And every time the department wants new equipment, the boss makes a big fuss about spending the money. Also, each of our branches has problems different from all other branches because of climate, geography, competition, or other factors.

## THE FOUR STAGES OF A SERVICE
## PERSON'S DEVELOPMENT

In talking to service people who work for many different companies around the United States and in other countries, it is obvious that they have a lot in common, one of which is the four stages most service people go through during their development. Let's call the first stage *idealism*. He took the test, attended training school, and was assigned to a territory in the local office. He thinks of his company as a giant of efficiency in a marvelous undertaking. Everything is done perfectly and everyone understands him and his particular problem. Many things are at his command and he's awed and impressed. He relies on the greatness and perfection of the company to the point where any derogatory remark about it—even from a customer—is a personal insult. He may not realize it then, but from this high point he is about to enter the most depressing phase of his career, a phase we'll call *disillusionment*.

He now begins to see the imperfections and inefficiencies of the company. He cannot understand how management can be so inefficient, shortsighted, heartless, and just plain dumb and still stay in business. Even minor errors in judgment, wastefulness, and unfairness become formidable. He cannot believe the lack of understanding of the real business needs on the part of his associates, management, and all departments—particularly the order and shipping departments. For instance, he tells the people in the factory that he needs a part right away to get a customer back in service, and he is told to his dismay that they won't be able to ship it for 18 weeks!

Everything is wrong. And what's worse, nobody will allow him to make it operate the right way. They won't accept the ideas he knows are right. The letter he wrote to somebody in the home office about a misplaced order brought back a dumb reply, and he wonders what kind of a company would keep such a jerk. He complains to the boss about all these problems, but he still goes along and tries. He either reaches the next stage soon, or gives up and takes a job with another company. If he does give up at this point he'll probably wander from one job to another for years. Most people outgrow this stage, retain some of their ideals, and enter the third stage of their career, which we'll call *enlightenment*.

By now he has begun to realize the value of expediency and compromise in dealing with associates and that they too are human beings. He also realizes that 52 times out of a hundred he may have been wrong. The value of the other departments in the company is becoming more apparent, and he is surprised to discover that other people have their own ideas, beliefs, troubles, and pride. He finds that not all people are equally capable, industrious, conscientious, or even honest, and that they never will be. There are superior, average, and poor employees, and any other company will be the same, because people are human everywhere. He's beginning to accept the fact that management people may not be perfect—they have their own particular problems and are usually honestly doing their best within their own limits of experience and ability, and with the people and facilities available to them. He's learned that his company is not a machine; it is a group of people working together cooperatively for a common purpose—the sale and service of a product at a profit to all concerned.

His profit is in the form of salary, prestige, satisfaction with the job he's doing, and a personal feeling of accomplishment. The customer's profit is in the form of a useful product at a reasonable cost. The management's profit is the same as his—money, prestige, satisfaction, and accomplishment. He's learned the value of his own work and the part it plays in connection with the work of others. He's learned the value of tolerance and understanding, the necessity for procedures and regulations, and the importance of the work of associates such as salesmen, accountants, office managers, and others who are not service engineers. He knows that he can't do it alone but that together the people can and do accomplish the job successfully. He now belongs—perhaps not as idealistically as when he began, but his enthusiasm is now much more valuable. He's a recognized part of the organization, and contributes his work as part of a team. This is the rewarding part of his career and although he may not yet be at the peak of his earning power, he is ready for the fourth and final part of his career, which we'll call *realism*.

Now he's a vital, smooth, working part of the organization. He may or may not be a supervisor or manager, but he is definitely responsible for a large chunk of business and has a wealth of facilities and people at his command. Everyone is helping in some manner and he's helping others. He listens to the other person's viewpoint, evaluates it as it is related to his own, and then acts decisively. He finds it necessary to make compromises every day. He realizes that modern industry is complex and requires a well-integrated team of engineers, accountants, toolmakers, buyers, salespeople, and service people, and he respects each one for his knowledge of his particular field.

Most importantly, he has learned to make decisions every day without endless argument on the pros and cons of the situation—and without realizing it, he's teaching less experienced people to do the same thing.

He's one of the people to whom new employees go for experience and guidance. People like to work with him and if he's overruled or his ideas are rejected, he doesn't sulk and brood for days. He's happy, respected, and part of the team. Above all, he's tolerant of others because he knows that he is not perfect himself. The best part of his business career and many opportunities for advancement with his company are still ahead of him.

Some people move quite rapidly through these four phases of development, although for others it takes five to ten years. Some never reach the maturity and human understanding, the power of expression, cooperativeness, and compromise combined with drive and efficiency required to continue to advance within an organization. Examine some of the people in your company whom you think are successful—successful not only in title or position, but because they lead full and rich lives, have gained the respect of their associates, and (what is most important) are able to respect themselves. You can see how they have shaken off the deadly disillusionment that can wither a career before it really gets started. You can see how they have gone through the enlightenment stage of their development and have learned the greatest lesson to be learned in this life: that people are human.

I think you'll find that when you examine these successful people, that above all they are realists. They know when to compromise and when not to compromise. They know that although they are only part of the whole team they're essential to it. They know their unique individual worth and how to get the most out of it, and from all this comes self-respect. They belong! Look at them and then take a good look at yourself to see how you shape up in comparison.

## SERVICE PEOPLE: THE BEST SOURCE OF CUSTOMER SATISFACTION

Another thing common to service people everywhere: they are without doubt the best source of repeat sales and happy, satisfied customers. The salesperson sees a customer when he or she sells something (perhaps several times on a large sale), and he or she may even call on the customer after the sale to see if the customer needs something else. But the service person sees the customer all the time in the customer's own environment. He or she performs the preventive maintenance, the repairs, and the emergency service. He or she listens to the complaints, makes sure that the product gives the customer what he expected to get, and in some cases helps the customer to understand what the product offers. The service engineer is the one who is there on weekends, holidays, and at 3:00 A.M. getting things going again after a failure.

If a customer decides to buy a competitor's equipment, the chances are that it's not because of something the salesperson said. It may be because of price, if there's enough of a difference, but most of the time when a customer changes manufacturers, it's either because the machine didn't work the way he thought it should or he didn't get what he considered to be good service. Many times a machine's working up to a customer's expectations is the result of a good service engineer who combines the actual operations capacity of the machine with the customer's expectations and comes up with a result that the customer can accept. A very high percentage of unhappy customers can be won back by a service engineer who handles the situation properly. It's important of course for a service engineer to feed this information to management and the sales department so that they can react properly, too.

There's another thing that's common to all service people: the image of the job. It takes real expertise to be able to repair today's complicated systems, and everybody is getting to be aware of it—management, customers, and fellow employees in other departments. Service is a respectable industry in its own right. It's necessary, profitable, and complicated, and it takes good people to run it.

The greatest frustration and the biggest customer complaint is having the same problem occur more than once. This is a tough problem but it has to be solved somehow. It's true that we now have highly sophisticated diagnostic tools to assure better analysis of whatever type of equipment we're responsible for, but we still need human beings to do it. The doctor, the lawyer, and the engineer constantly try to obtain additional knowledge of their professions so they can cut down their percentage of errors. Professional service engineers must always be hungry for new knowledge in the field to cut down their percentage of errors.

## THE SKILL LEVEL CONCEPT

A major factor to be considered in developing a technical field force is the skill levels required to perform the necessary work. Let's say that your company sells and services commercial packaging equipment and systems. In servicing the equipment, some of the work functions required might include leveling conveyors, cleaning and lubrication, system troubleshooting, electrical repair, welding, analysis and repair of electronic systems, and adjustment and replacement of drive belts.

Any and all of these functions, and many others, may

be required to be performed both during preventive maintenance and in repairing breakdowns. Some are required on a scheduled basis, and some only when catastrophes occur. When you consider the different skill levels required for these and for the other tasks involved, you will surely agree that having any one person qualified to perform all these tasks, and perform them well, would be difficult indeed.

For one thing, life is so complicated these days that the jack-of-all-trades has just about disappeared, and there is some doubt whether he ever really existed. You must also ask yourself whether you can afford the expense of trying to train any one person to do everything. You must also consider whether people are really interested in doing everything. A highly trained solid state electronics expert may have a difficult time maintaining interest in greasing rollers on conveyor belts. The odds are that he will perform these tasks for you from time to time if you ask him to, but since it is not really what he likes to do, he may not do it very well. All you have really accomplished if you force the issue is that you are both dissatisfied with the results.

People are proudest of their performance when they are doing an outstanding job of what they are best qualified to do. Over the years I have often had the very pleasant task of talking to newly hired service people in their first training class. When it comes time for them to ask questions, someone always wants to know what the possibilities are for advancement and how long it will take before they are recognized. I always told them that advancement was up to them, that advancements were made on the basis of merit and capability; that promotions were not always given to salespeople, or to administrative people, or to service people, but to those who were doing well at what they were assigned to at the time. I also told them that although they could aspire to sales, management, supervision, or whatever else was of interest to them in the future, they did not need to go those routes to be successful. I emphasized that whether or not they were successful was their decision alone, and was not based on the opinions of friends and neighbors. If you were hired as a service person, and retired secure in the knowledge that you were the best service person the company ever had, then you were surely successful.

The ideal situation, then, is for you to have several grades of service people, each qualified to perform a specific level of service for your customers. Each needs only the training and tools required to be able to perform those specific services, as well as a salary that is fair and equitable.

If you are starting a service business, it will be quite simple to begin this way and establish your precedents. If you have been in business for a while and your practice over the years has been to hire one grade of serviceman and expect him to perform at all levels of basic and sophisticated service, you may face a difficult transition to this new way of doing things. As noted before, change is generally looked upon as something frightening that will destroy things as they are. Here's where you are in the sales business again. The concept has to be sold to the troops! If it is merely pinned up on the bulletin board, you can be sure that it will not be well received, and that it will never work. The reason for this is that your service people will not really understand what you are trying to do, and they will therefore resist the changes you are trying to make.

Let's assume that you have a group of service people —all highly trained and well paid—who have been with you for several years. Their pay is based on their experience and capabilities, which are considerable. Since the services you perform go from cleaning and greasing to repairing very complicated electronic equipment, you may be having some difficulty getting the basic work done. They do it when they have to, but it is far from their field of interest and they usually perform these duties in a hurry and not too well. You have carefully broached the subject of another job grade before, and although they made no specific statements, you had the feeling they were afraid of it, and therefore were against it. You have developed on paper a job grade for the "greasemonkey" work, have decided upon a proper pay scale, and have even gone so far as to hire someone who is reporting for work next Monday morning. You have set up a meeting for all your service people on Friday afternoon. What will you tell them?

You let them know that you appreciate the work they have been doing over the years, even when it included tasks they did not really like to perform. But they always came through, and you appreciate it. But now, you say, you'd like to try a new way of dealing with this problem of having skilled, experienced people do basic tasks.

You discuss your idea of setting up a different service grade whose required qualifications are the basic tasks that you perform as a part of your total service package. People can be hired and trained to perform these functions and these functions only. You assure your service people that there is enough work on the books so that this will definitely not be a threat to them, but will be an addition to the staff. They are certainly aware that this basic service work has been neglected anyway because of the heavy workload, and that it is an important part of service to the customers.

You tell them that when the new person starts (notice how smoothly you can shift gears from the person you will hire someday to the new person about to start) he or she will be training for a short time, and will then go on the road. This person will no doubt have to make some trips to customer sites with them to become familiar with the equipment locations and other important things, and you know you can depend on them to help.

Then you can emphasize that as soon as the new person can become productive, they (the established engineers) will no longer have to do the basic maintenance jobs they have been required to do in the past, but can spend their efforts on the more complicated tasks which require all their experience and know-how.

Although your people will undoubtedly go for this pitch, they will not have been sold a bill of goods, because everything you said was true. They will be able to spend their time doing the things they were trained to do, and do them better. The basic work will be done now by a service person who is trained and qualified to perform those precise tasks, and will therefore be accomplished in a professional and conscientious manner. You will get the basic work performed by a person who is on a lower pay scale than the experts (who were overqualified for the work anyway), and this will improve your cost ratios. Since *all* the work will now be done more professionally, your customers will be happier. When your customers are happier, they will buy more services, and you will be able to hire more service people of both grades. So it works out well for everyone.

## WHERE TO FIND FIELD SERVICE PEOPLE

Potential service people are usually found in all sorts of places, from service stations to college graduating classes. Service businesses that demand handling very sophisticated equipment require that all service people have engineering degrees. In the past 20 years or so, some companies have changed their policies several times from preferring college graduates to favoring mechanics or trade-school graduates and back to college graduates. If you buy the "appropriate skill" philosophy, you must logically agree that you will find different kinds of service people in different places.

Remember, locating and hiring an adequate number of service people to fix things for customers is not your only requirement. You also have to think about where you will find your future field supervisors and managers. You will of course hire many service people who have no other aspiration than to be a good service person, but you will also have some who have their eyes on, first, their boss's job, and then perhaps yours.

If you need people for the most basic jobs (the cleaning, oiling, greasing, and adjustment we discussed before), you should perhaps cover the trade schools, the vocational and technical schools, and the high schools. Find people who like to work with their hands, who like to learn things, and who like to move from place to place. If they have the desire, they will be able to advance—first into more technical and more demanding service positions, and then into supervision and management. I have seen some people who did an outstanding job after being hired directly from a corner filling station where they greased cars and changed tires. The basic jobs are a good way to learn service performance from the ground up.

Don't fall into the trap of looking at these basic jobs as being beneath the average person; they are not. Assuming that you are paying a competitive salary, and perhaps a bit more, consider what you are really offering a young person who has little or no experience: a job with the opportunity to learn; good pay and a full benefit package; travel, at least in your service area;

a company vehicle to drive; and uniforms and other such benefits.

That's not a bad deal for someone who's just starting out.

When you consider the other more technical jobs, you have to look in other places. Young people just out of the military, but trained in your particular specialty, are and have always been good candidates. They have been around for a while, have had excellent training, and are eager to get a start in civilian life. Trade schools that offer training in your specialty are other good sources of service people. And there are always your competitors, although you must realize that hiring from competitors works both ways: hiring a person here and there is not so bad, but if you should develop the reputation of pirating from competitors, they will surely do it to you, too. But you should always look at associated businesses as a good source of people, and if your working climate is good, the word will get around and you will rarely have to advertise.

There's another source you should consider, although it is not really a source of permanent service people. When you hire people in sales, an excellent way for them to learn the products they will sell is to perform that service for a while. I remember several men I hired for future assignment to sales, who, after a year as servicemen, made outstanding salesmen, and later just as outstanding supervisors and managers, simply because they understood the business!

## THE SPECIAL NEEDS OF FIELD SERVICE PEOPLE

Field service people have the same needs as other people—basic needs for food, clothing, and shelter and intangible needs for recognition and status—but they sometimes express these needs in a different way. Most field people really like it out there. They like working on a different machine or system in a different place every day. They like driving from one place to another to get their work done, and sometimes resent being cooped up in an office. As a rule they have a violent distaste for paperwork and at times must be driven to complete even the simplest expense and service reports. They have a feeling about their work that is sometimes hard for others to understand. They will work extra hours and even go to the job on weekends for the sheer thrill of changing whatever they are working on from an inanimate piece of scrap iron into a working system that delights the eye and ear. To them nothing sounds better than a properly running diesel, or an air conditioning compressor being loaded, or a computer clicking and humming. Sometimes it gets to be almost an obsession to really fix something that the customer says has never worked right since he got it. If you have never been a service person yourself, this may all sound rather strange, but it is true. Field service people take a great deal of pride in their work, and managers sometimes have a tendency to take advantage of this quality.

Earlier I mentioned the prevailing attitude in many companies about the service people: they are seen as ''the greasy-fingered people in the back room.'' Unfortunately, a similar problem exists in many service businesses between the service people and the rest of the employees. This is particularly true when the service business in question actively sells its services and has a sales staff. This atttude doesn't exist because of any kind of prejudice, or because it was developed on purpose, but it's one of those things that we should fight.

The one group of people that most needs to be motivated is the sales force. Salespeople have to be given *reasons* to sell; they have to be continually raised to a level of excitement; they have to be motivated with contests, prizes, and gimmicks. And these efforts do pay off in the sales business. But other people also need some of the same treatment. Perhaps we need a bumper sticker that says, "Love a service person." For many years I have been a serviceman, and have been closely associated with that end of the business. Very often the people performing the services we sell are, in their mind at least, not really part of the group. It's also unfortunate that this attitude extends to the field supervisors in the operational area. The point is that to a large degree they feel neglected, and when they feel that way, it might as well be true.

It isn't usually a matter of salary, since pay is generally quite competitive these days wherever you go; it's that salespeople have to be motivated but operational people are assumed to be self-starters, and many of them aren't. We take advantage of their affection for the performance of their work, and act as if they were born with a motivational gland in their throats. Because when you get right down to it, there's really no such thing as a self-starter; there are people who are proud of their work and may require only minimal supervision, and we have a tendency to call them self-starters. Actually, they need as much motivation as anyone else, and if they don't get it, you may find yourself wondering why they have gone into a gradual decline.

As I've said, it isn't usually a matter of salary. As a group service people are somewhat less aggressive than salespeople, and this can cause them to be neglected when it comes to salary increases. In general, though, they are probably not significantly underpaid; it's the extras that count. Salespeople get incentive or bonus pay, and service people don't. I'm not necessarily saying that they should, but consider that salespeople are in a higher salary bracket to start with, so their merit raises are larger. In addition, they get bonuses or incentives. All of this is based on their delivery of satisfactory performance. The service person is also expected to deliver satisfactory performance, but for less money. This is not necessarily inequitable, nor have I ever felt that all should be reimbursed equally. But on the other hand, look at it this way: a package of your services is somehow sold to a customer, and now the services must be performed. Neither the sales nor the performance is of any value without the other.

Then there is the matter of recognition. All people like to be recognized by their peers, their superiors, their friends, and their families for what they do, and that is the justification for spending money on award trips for the sales force. Various companies call them different things: Man of the Year, Million Dollar Club, Presidents' Club. These awards are a valid method of rewarding outstanding sales performance. It therefore makes sense to give similar rewards to outstanding people in the service field. The service person spends much more time each day under the direct eye of the customer than the salesperson ever does. In talking to the customer before and after the service is performed, he can do the company an enormous amount of good. Many times the initial sale by a salesperson has been followed by subsequent sales to that specific customer as a result of the service person's work performance, personality, and sales efforts.

As a service organization comes into existence and first becomes aware that services can actually be sold for profit, the sales function usually rests with the service people themselves. As the business matures, and at the proper point of business growth, the sales and performance functions are split so that each can be more productive. But the service person will always be one of your best salespeople by virtue of his or her performance and direct customer contact.

I am suggesting, therefore, that you set up an effective recognition system for your technical staff. It must be done in such a manner that all grades of service people have an opportunity to share in the benefits, and should have all the same award levels you have for the salespeople: monthly or quarterly bulletins, office plaques, personal awards, pictures in the company paper, and so on. You'll have a problem with the mechanics of selecting the winners, since operational performance is more difficult to measure than sales volume.

But this problem can be solved in many cases by the use of a subjective method of evaluation such as having your field managers submit recommendations for outstanding performers. There are two drawbacks to this approach, however. First, it will at times be almost impossible to get your field managers to write letters of recommendation. Second, they'll have a natural tendency to write the letters about the performers working on the largest jobs, with the most sophisticated equipment, or with the largest customers. When this happens, the young service person located in Chugwater, Wyoming, who is really outstanding when you consider his actual and expected performance, will feel that he can't ever make the awards list until he gets a transfer to the Chicago office and learns solid state electronics.

I have always thought that any field manager worth his salt must have at least one person on his staff who has done something very well, and should be recognized for it. If he doesn't, it is either because he actually doesn't have any good performers (which reflects on his management capability) or he just can't find the time to write a letter about them (which reflects even more on his management skills).

A bone of contention among the operational performers in many companies is the lack of meetings. While they see the salespeople going to meetings all the time, the company just doesn't seem to see a need to pass information along to them. The point here is not that there should be as many meetings for one group of employees as for another just so that it will be equal, but that there is always a need to inform people about changes in policy or procedure, new products, new tools or servicing techniques, and you should plan to pass this information along in a meeting rather than in the form of memos or printed matter in their mailboxes. There is also considerable benefit to be gained from getting people together and letting them exchange information.

## FOLLOW-UP TRAINING

One facet of developing a service person that deserves very special attention is training. I'm sure we can all agree that basic training in what you manufacture and how it is serviced is, or at least should be, a primary part of the hiring and orientation cycle (see Chapter 7). It's the training that follows that requires our attention—the ongoing, follow-up training that should be a constant part of their lives.

I've said before that service people are proud of their performance and that they can somehow survive with very little assistance from others. If information is not available to them, they will spend hours figuring out how to make something work. Although this is a highly commendable attitude, it is costly. If the people on your service staff are to be really effective, they should have the necessary information at their fingertips so that they can spend a minimum amount of time searching for the right answers. The process of passing this data on to them can be classified as training, and also as giving them the proper tools.

For instance, the printing of lots of service data sheets seems at times to be one of the ideal places to reduce overhead. The real cost, however, is not in the printing, but in the development and arrangement. All field people need information about how things work, where to get parts, what parts are available, calibration techniques, and so on. Since customers who perform their own service need the same information, we can develop a data file that will perform the same function for both users. The secret is giving them this wonderful training aid in the best possible form, so that they can select the particular data they need and proceed with their work.

Sheets and manuals of this type are usually designed by factory engineers who have not been in the field, so that they are more like manufacturing instructions than field service data sheets. They should be written by the engineers, laid out by the artists, and given final review by the user group. (By final review I mean that they should be gone through word for word by an experienced service person to see if it is arranged properly, whether field terminology is used, whether the information required is there, and whether it can be easily translated into action.)

There is another kind of training that is important: as new products find their way into your line, there will be a lot of literature produced for the sales group and for the customer. As the product finds its way into the field and then into the hands of the customers, remember that the first one delivered is a potential service problem. It can fail on its first day in service, and require replacement or repair. When this happens, it will be most helpful to have the service data in the hands of the field people.

The argument is frequently put forth that the only way you can find out how to service a unit is to wait until it has been in the field for a while, and then write up the sheets from experience. The difficulty with this method is that by the time you get the sheets written and distributed, the field people will have given up in disgust and will have replaced the units with something they understand. At the very least they will have developed their own methods for easy repair, which may very well either keep the product from ever being a real success or may simply reflect extremely high repair cost. You may feel that all this talk of service data sheets does not really belong in a chapter about the care and feeding of field personnel, but it does. It is important to their performance, and while it may possibly not be classified as a true motivator, it is surely a demotivator when it is not properly handled.

There are also follow-up training courses to be considered. These are the packaged courses that cover all sorts of subjects and are sent to the field offices to be used either in groups or by individuals. They can be considered ongoing training on subjects that can be covered in an hour or so, and therefore do not require the transportation of the field people to a training center. They can either be on selected parts of your product line or on related subjects that are useful. This approach to training is particularly useful in the areas that your ordinary training does not cover, the wide field of expertise that is ordinarily felt to be covered by "experience" and "the school of hard knocks." If you can find someone who has the necessary skills to put these subjects on paper in a manner acceptable to the eyes and ears of the users, you will have a real gold mine.

Like anyone else, field people are turned on by training, by learning how to do their jobs better, by knowing that you are interested in their progress, and by understanding that if they move to a better job (or at least a different one) there will be information there waiting for them. It's not enough, however, to have the courses and training materials printed and waiting for distribution; to be useful, they have to be *used*. Because of the day-to-day pressure of getting the work done, the odds are that your field managers will tend to neglect this all-important area. The only way you can improve the skills of your people is to ensure that they are given not only the training materials, but the motivation and the opportunity to use them for their advantage and yours.

## IMAGE, ADVANCEMENT, TOOLS, AND SUPPORT

What about a service person's image? He does have one, both to himself and to the customer. When I first became a serviceman, the work was associated with equipment that at times could be exceptionally dirty. It was easy to see that there were two basic types of servicemen: those who looked as if they had been cleaning boilers all day (which may very well have been the case) and those who looked neat and clean at all times, except for the moments when they were actually inside the boiler.

The secret is to dress neatly, based on the need of

the industry. Whether a suit and tie or a shirt and slacks combination will be acceptable depends on custom, how you and the customers feel about it, the climate, and to a degree the part of the country in which the person is working. Whatever he does wear, though, should be neat and clean. He can either wear your uniform or street clothes, but he must give the right impression to the customer when he appears. If the work he does is dirty, he can then put on a pair of coveralls and perform the work. (I used to supply myself with white coveralls, sometimes even at my own expense if necessary.) After the work is complete, and he is supposed to meet the customer again and explain what he has done, he can remove the coveralls and again look like a proper representative of your business. This will improve not only the company's image, but also his own.

Tools can be anything from screwdrivers to training manuals, from trucks to oscilloscopes, from uniforms to hard hats. My personal philosophy has always been that money spent on the proper high-quality tools is money well spent. If you purchase for your field people the cheapest tools possible, they will be aware of this immediately and will perform their tasks cheaply. Remember that your only real assets in the service business are people and skills. It becomes apparent, then, that if you equip them with the tools to do their work as effectively as possible, and in as short a time as possible, they will do a better job for you. Also, people do better when they work with tools they are proud of, and customers are favorably impressed by a serviceman who has the tools he needs to do the work. Broken tools and instruments held together with tape are just not very impressive.

In these days of automation and instrumentation,

some tasks can be properly performed only with the proper tools. Let's face it: an electronic temperature indicator is faster and more accurate than a mercury thermometer, and you just can't measure small tolerances with a yardstick. Also, using modern technology, you can perform functions for your customers that you could not have done previously, or that would have cost much more. It is much to your advantage to give your field people the capability of performing their work more effectively for both you and the customer, and in having them know that they are effective.

Although it is important for your field people to feel that their jobs are important, and that they can be successful by staying in their positions, they also must see the possibility—even the probability—of promotion. Ordinarily, your field service supervisors will be promoted from the ranks of service people. There will be higher grades of service jobs to aspire to. There are two reasons, however, that you should constantly search the ranks of your service people for those having management potential. First, they are a source of excellent people, and those who have the ability deserve the opportunity to be promoted. This also provides them with hope for the future when they see one of their own people make it. Second, you should also try to get the proper balance of experience in your management ranks, and this makes it worthwhile to look for operations people to promote. If all your managers are from the sales area (the most likely place for your selections), you will over a period of years lose some of the diversity and excitement that a variety of backgrounds can give you.

It was mentioned earlier that the service person should be able to retire proudly as a service person, with a strong feeling of having been successful. But he can only do this if you create the proper climate. It's easy to say that some people just don't want to be supervisors, and to let them go along in their job from year to year. What is needed is a way to recognize such people for what they really are—extremely valuable employees with priceless experience, who can perform their work in an outstanding manner. They most likely have a loyal following of customers who will call your dispatcher and say things like, "I need service right away, and I understand that Pete is out of town on another call, but if he isn't available I'll wait until he is. Put me first on his list when he returns." Customers don't act that way just because Pete is a nice guy, but because he understands their problems and knows how to solve them. They have faith in what he says and does. He is one of your best assets, and should be treated as such. It's your responsibility to find ways to repay him, to give him the recognition that he deserves, and to motivate him to continue along his successful path.

We can talk in more detail about motivation and meeting the needs of your service people, but except for the differencs I have noted, which are largely a matter of emphasis, they are the same as for others. In the previous chapter on building field managers, motivation was covered in considerable depth, and the basic philosophy is the same: it really is a matter of support. Your field force is your real asset, and it is important that they feel this in your attitudes toward them. It is important that they realize how you feel about them and their performance.

I feel very strongly that if we as managers have ever had an opportunity to improve the effectiveness of our businesses, it has been in the area of making our service performers into professionals—professionals in the way they look, in the way they talk, in the way they feel, and of course in the way they accomplish their tasks. It is too easy to fall into the trap of looking at them as mechanics, even though they may be servicing the most advanced and sophisticated equipment. All we really have to do is treat them as professionals, give them the necessary tools to allow them to perform as professionals, and support them as professionals.

# 9

## Selling service

WHETHER OR NOT you are a profit center, and whether or not you sell your services to customers, you are in the business of selling service. It's most obvious, of course, when you sell service to customers, although it is perhaps not so obvious that you are in the business of selling service every day to your management. This was discussed in Chapter 1, but it deserves some additional emphasis.

Without involving ourselves in a sales course, let's look at why I have termed this "selling." People don't buy anything unless it has been sold to them. If you purchase a tube of shaving cream, you can be sure that the manufacturers have sold it to you on the basis of their reputation, their advertising, or your experience with the product. What really counts is *why* people buy. They buy things because they need them, but they choose a particular product over others because of the features, the functions, and the benefits of that product. We can study thousands of pages of sales manuals, and attend numerous sales training courses, but in the final assessment it always boils down to *features, functions,* and *benefits.* This is true of everything people buy, including ideas, proposals, programs, and suggestions (and even recommendations that they should approve enough money in the budget for you to expand your service department and its functions).

The features and the functions are important, and if you understand the product you are selling they can be easily and fully explained. It's the area of benefits where the difficult job begins. Benefits are very specific. When they are business benefits they can be divided into those that make or save money, provide more effective use of time, improve products, and improve the health and safety of employees.

## SELLING SERVICE TO YOUR BOSS

Whenever you are selling an idea to your boss, the benefits are not only important; they are the primary reason for your getting approval. Do not, however, forget the personal benefits that may very well affect the decision of your boss. Recognition, for one—perhaps as a result of adopting an outstanding program, and for being an advanced thinker. Perhaps he can write an article for a trade magazine. Perhaps you will provide added security for his job. He may get a raise, or perhaps a letter of commendation from his boss.

Your boss will not implement your idea just because it's a good one, or just because it's your idea. He will buy the idea and put it into effect if you sell him on the benefits to the company and to himself. You have to approach this sale like any other—with understanding, preparation, and resolve. You have to be sincerely convinced that the idea is valid, and that the benefits are realistic. You have to know your boss and what turns him on. And you have to be prepared. Remember, you are making a sale to your most important customer, so your presentation must be well prepared and presented in a highly professional manner. There's something else to remember, and it's one of the primary principles of sales: you are in the business of changing people's minds—in this case, the boss's.

Mind changing means teaching and learning. The degree to which you see a change in the behavior of your boss is a measure of what he has learned from you. Also, we change our minds only when we want to. The amount of mind changing going on is the result of how much he learns multiplied by his interest. If you get him interested, you'll change his mind. The whole mind-changing process is emotional rather than intellectual. We don't like to change, so when we do, there must have been a good reason to do so. This is usually experienced as an emotion, a hope, a challenge, a longing, or an excitement. If you think about this for a moment, you'll realize that the mind changing takes place within the person, and that in order to change, he or she needs to be involved, to discuss, to analyze, to challenge, to create, to reconstruct his or her ideas and thinking. That kind of reconstruction is a serious matter. But if your ideas are good, and you believe in them, and you make the effort to present them well, you will change that person's mind, and he or she will buy.

## SELLING SERVICE TO THE PUBLIC

There are service businesses that perform warranty service only, those that perform service for customers who walk in off the street, and those that perform service in a thousand other ways. Here I am referring to those who sell their service to the public—services performed on either the product manufactured by the company or on other products. Services sold are generally either on a contract basis, a "you call and we'll come fix it" basis, or some combination of the two. Usually the contract arrangement calls for the service company to provide any or all of the following services: routine labor for preventive maintenance, emergency labor to correct breakdowns, and parts and materials used.

Selling this kind of service is a world away from selling a product. It is selling a concept, selling an idea, and in many cases selling a need of which the customer may be initially unaware. People in general are just beginning to be aware of the concept of preventive maintenance—that it is far more cost-effective in the long run to maintain equipment in peak condition and thus to a great degree prevent failures and breakdowns. But there are many in the service business who have not yet been convinced that preventive maintenance is the answer to the problems of our customers: the problem of never knowing how much maintenance will cost each year, of paying for a catastrophic failure that could have been prevented, or of having costly machinery fail long before its anticipated time of obsolescence.

When you are selling the concept of maintenance (in whatever specific form it may take), you will need what I have called the concept salesperson. Such a salesperson will need the capabilities of any highly professional salesperson, such as the ability to prospect for customers, to qualify them as buyers, to answer their objections, and to know how to get their orders. Such salespeople should be able to operate quite satisfactorily with a somewhat limited knowledge of the details of your business. In other words, at the start of their selling careers they should not require the years of experience it would take them to be able to answer most of the technical questions customers can ask. While they are getting this experience, they can always find others in the organization from whom to ask help.

If you are selling the repair and modernization of older and perhaps obsolete equipment, you will have a need for the experienced salesperson. In these areas, it is not only necessary to be able to answer the questions the customers will inevitably ask, but a certain amount of experience is required for the salesperson to be able to recognize what must be done, and be able to price it intelligently.

In many companies it has often been believed that the only way to develop salespeople with this type of experience is to wait the years necessary for them to build the knowledge the hard way. Training a young salesperson in the technicalities is thought to take so long and to be so unproductive (and usually so boring to the student) that it is considered impractical. This, in my opinion, is not the case, and the problem lies in the training itself. Many times our concept of such training is of a slightly rewritten version of the training package that is made available to the service people and engineers. But what is really required is the development of a technical course of training for the salesperson, rather than a rearrangement. If the skills required by a technical salesperson were to be analyzed, and the training were to be developed to satisfy those and only those requirements, the job could be done in a reasonable time. The point is that the salesperson does not need to know and understand the intricate workings of each part of the system; rather, he or she has to understand the needs of the system as a whole, what it is supposed to do, and what parts are required to allow it to perform its function. When used in the development of technical training for salespeople, this concept can help make them effective in a relatively short time, and then allow them to gain more experience in the field.

After the salespeople have completed their formal training they can and should continue their technical training in the field. One way to accomplish this without the development of specialized courses is the use of the field courses you have developed for the service people. The salespeople, who don't require all the technical detail in such courses, can "skim" the course and take away what they need. Perhaps a study guide directing them to the parts that would be most interesting could be helpful. In some cases, it may be useful to have a field technical course presented to a group of salespeople by a field technical supervisor or by a service person who has expertise in that area.

As I have noted earlier, a skilled concept salesperson can be effective without extensive field experience or technical knowledge. It is also true that such salespeople will become more valuable as they learn more about the services they are selling. It is very definitely our responsibility to ensure that the necessary training be made available to them.

Any company has the ability to hire highly professional concept salespeople and to sell service contracts. The controlling fact of life is that without an operations group as professional as the sales force, you will very soon run out of customers. The selling of anything, particularly of a concept, must be very closely tied to performance: you have to sell what you can perform and perform what you sell. If you can do that, and constantly do everything you can to improve the effectiveness of both sales and operational groups, meeting your growth plans won't be your biggest problem; it will be convincing your management that the growth is real, that it is not a one-shot deal, that it is ongoing and will remain so, and that you need the proper financing to support the growth in the years to come. That is your biggest sales job!

## THE ART OF THE PRESENTATION

Making an effective presentation is, like almost anything else, a learnable skill. You can't really accomplish much without planning ahead and the first step, quite naturally, is to decide what your real objective is. When you consider the possible reasons for making a presentation, keep in mind that each may require a different approach, a different format, and a different technique. In each case, the needs of the audience may vary. Some of the possible general reasons for delivering a presentation could be to inform, to teach, and to persuade. Of course, it can be argued that these three possibilities are always present, but we will usually be able to select the primary reason. In many cases, our objective as managers will be persuasion, the gentle art of separating management from its funds.

### Choosing the medium of the presentation

But regardless of how the objective is selected, once it has been chosen, we can proceed to the next issue— the medium most appropriate for the presentation. This decision will be affected to a large degree by the size of the audience, as well as by the subject matter. A group of two, or of forty, may direct your choice to a desk flipchart, an easel flipchart, overhead transparencies, or 35 mm slides. Let's look at some of the advantages of each.

*Desk Flipchart.* This is generally a three-ring binder which folds over and stands on the desk of the "customer." The sheets are usually 8½" × 11" heavy paper on which you inscribe your message. This method of communication is ideal for an audience of one or two, but no more, or the members of the audience will have to crane their necks to see. Once they've done that two or three times, you've lost them.

*Easel Flipchart.* These are the rather large paper pads that clip to an easel. They are excellent for somewhat larger audiences, and have the advantage of flexibility in that you can write on your prepared pages as you proceed. The length of your presentation is a limiting factor, since it's cumbersome to have more pages than are available in one pad. The mechanics of changing pads in the middle of your presentation can also be very distracting.

*Overhead Transparencies.* These are excellent for a larger audience, because they can be projected on a large screen and, like the flipchart, can be written on as you go along. Projection can be done with a reasonable amount of ambient light, so a sleep-inducing dark room is not a necessity. There are some special techniques required, which will be discussed later in the chapter.

*35 mm Slides.* These are particularly good for the larger audience. There is more flexibility and specialized projection equipment available than for the other media. They are also excellent when you need action pictures. Slides ordinarily require a moderately dark room.

Another factor involved in your choice of media is whether or not there will be discussion and interaction with the audience. The flipcharts and overheads are good for this, since it's easier to go back and forth and to write on the sheets during the discussion. A 35 mm format is better for the more formal presentation with minimal discussion. Another factor is the kind of facilities available to you for preparation of artwork. Anyone who can print with some degree of neatness can make a flipchart, whereas transparencies and slides require a more professional touch.

### Producing the material for the presentation

After you have selected the most appropriate medium for your presentation, the next step is the actual production of the material.

*Flipcharts.* Print neatly and legibly. If you can't, find someone who can. Use colored marking pens. The tasteful use of color can direct the audience's attention to the words you want to emphasize. Use color on each page for emphasis, but avoid making each one look like a rainbow. It's entirely acceptable to use symbolic colors—green for approval or money, red for alarm or a negative feeling, blue for new ideas (blue sky). Put only key words on each page, and limit yourself to about ten of those. People aren't supposed to read the chart; they are supposed to listen to what you're saying. The chart is there only to attract their attention, and to emphasize important points. Print large so that the audience can read it. It's better to flip pages rapidly than to focus on one page for too long. Each page should have one idea only. Don't flip them so fast that the audience can't read them. Most flipchart pages are semiopaque, so print only on every other sheet. That way the audience won't be tempted to try to make out the faint outlines on the next page. When they're trying to see what's coming next, they will pay very little attention to what you are saying.

*Overhead Transparencies.* The same general ideas that were noted under flipcharts apply here—use large print, limit the number of words, and use color. No doubt you have been to presentations where the speaker projected on a screen a complete page from a book or perhaps a sheet with 70 columns of numbers. When you do this you either wait until the audience reads it all, read it to them, or wait until they have read part of it and then put on the next transparency. Whichever choice you make, you've blown it; it's better to just use the key words and tell them the rest. If they need all the details, give them a handout at the end of the presentation. Use color. You can purchase wonderful kits that will help you produce highly professional transparencies with charts, graphs, and curves. With the proper kind of copy machine, you can make full-color transparencies from magazine illustrations, 35 mm slides, and so on. If you don't have such a machine, the copy machine representative in your city probably will, and will make your transparencies for you at a price. An in-house art and advertising department can also produce some beautiful work for you. Use overlays to tell a story step by step, so you can build up suspense and hold the audience's interest until the end.

*35 mm Slides.* You can use slides made by others, have them produced by your art department, or use a camera yourself and get just the shots you want. Once again, limit the words. If you are going to use a dual-projection fader to really impress people, be sure to have your slides mounted and registered very carefully. When you take camera in hand to do your own, remember that film is much less expensive than a return trip to Peoria. Take a lot from all angles, and bracket the exposures on every shot so there will always be one that will project well. A lot of "insurance" shots are a good idea—even the world's great photographers do it.

Here are a few points about production in general. First, start early—don't wait until three days before your appointment with the Board of Directors to start throwing a presentation together. Plan it out so you can decide what you need in the way of art work. Then, while all of that is in production, you can get to work on your script. As you write it, say it out loud. You have to remember that you will be speaking the words, so it must be written with that in mind. The written word is very formal, and you should never say things the way you ordinarily write them. Try using your latest policy bulletin as a script some day, and see how artificial and stilted it sounds when spoken.

## The actual presentation

Now we are ready for the final step, the actual presentation itself. Here are a few specific technical points:

□ Check your equipment several times. Make sure you have a spare projector bulb and an extension cord that will reach far enough, and make sure that the slides are not in the tray upside down. Then check it again.

□ *Never, never, never* show a blank screen. When using overheads, turn the projector on when you want them to see the slide, and then turn it off! Go from one transparency to the next with the projector off. A blank screen with the light on is irritating, and since the people in the audience may not realize what's making them feel that way, they will get irritated at you. (After all, you are the person standing in the front of the room.) When using 35 mm slides, use blank slides in the proper places to keep from ever having a bright screen. Either learn to operate the projector properly or train an assistant.

□ If you feel you must use a pointer, don't. If you are adamant on this point, you can use a pointer on overheads, but use a pencil on the projector, not a long pointer on the screen. If you think you need a pointer, you may really just need a better slide.

□ Position the screen properly so that everyone can see it. And don't assume this; have a few helpers sit in some of the chairs and sit behind them to check it out. Sometimes the screen is better placed at the front corner of the room, at an angle, rather than directly facing the audience.

□ Check everything about three more times.

When your preparations are all made, and the final materials are in hand, it's time to start practicing. It's not an exaggeration to say that this is the most important part of all. Any presentation worth doing at all is worth doing well, and the only way to have it succeed professionally is to practice.

When you practice, do it aloud, and each time you go through your script, change it as necessary to be sure it "speaks" well and that you are comfortable with each word. Time your slides so that you don't leave them on for more than 15 to 20 seconds. If you have a lot of words that take longer than that, turn the projector off or use a blank slide.

Keep going through your presentation until you are tired of hearing it. That way, when something goes wrong, you will be ready. Be prepared with something to say if the power goes off or if the projector blows up.

If someone has kicked the power cord out of the receptacle, walk back and plug it in, but have something appropriate to say while you're doing it. Your audience may remember your victorious brush with adversity far longer than they remember what your presentation was about!

The presentation is extremely important. Many times very large business decisions may hang in the balance, dependent on how the chairman accepts your program. It's worth your attention and your time. The end result of your presentation quality is your personal reputation, and the success of your service business.

# 10

# Measuring results and making profits

THE RESULTS of your efforts can be measured both objectively and subjectively, and you will find it necessary to do both. Objective measurement is best accomplished with numbers. If you are doing your accounting by hand, they will be hard to come by sometimes, but they are available. If you are using computers, the numbers will be plentiful.

The most obvious measurements are sales, costs, profit, and growth. These are simple to read on a statement, and don't require a lot of interpretation. But the purpose of measuring results is to evaluate your actual performance compared with your plan, and to see whether you are on the way to accomplishing your objectives. Therefore you must display your plan and your actual performance, so you can immediately note any variances.

But that's not enough; you must also display what has been called the first step to exception reporting—trend reporting (see Chapter 5). Since trends will be plotted by most managers anyway, it makes sense to provide the information to them and to yourself within the reporting system. To use cost as an example, there is surely one of your cost ratios that bothers you each month, and this causes you to push your field managers each month. As a result of this prodding, they start keeping that specific cost plotted on a curve, so they can easily answer your questions when you ask them each month. What they are really doing is plotting a trend. If the cost of their operation appears to be going upward, they will notice this at once, and can then investigate the cause. In any event they will be prepared for your call.

If it's that important, you may wonder why it's realistic to make each manager plot the curve. You may of course consider it to be a valuable training aid, but if that's not the case, print that and any other important trends on your financial statements each month—billings per service person, for example, or perhaps sales per salesperson. They should not become a permanent part of your reporting, and need be printed only as long as they deserve high visibility. When the problem is put to rest, choose another trend and start printing that. After all, you're not liable to run out of trends or problems in the near future.

The subjective measurement of overall performance, or of performance in any specific area, is something else entirely. There are no numbers printed by the computer, no measurement criteria established by the comptroller. Here you're on your own. There are things you can look for, however, and things you can ask your people and your customers about.

One question you can ask is, what's the corporate image? Has it improved since your organization came into existence? Do your customers and the general

public look upon your company as being clean, rever-
ent, loyal, trustworthy, and brave? On the negative
side, if they don't think of you in those terms, why
don't they, and has your organization had anything to
do with their attitude? You can only learn these things
by asking, and no one could be a better person to ask
than your most vocal and critical customer. You may
already know what he will say, but if you hadn't at
one time or another given him cause for offense, he
woudn't feel as he does. Ask this customer what his
feelings are, and every time he starts to slow down,
ask him another leading question. When he is so tired
of complaining that even he starts to feel embarrassed,
you are getting to the important part. Although he may
have the most one-sided attitude in the world and he
may be basing his complaints on things you did to him
ten years ago, his past complaints may still be valid.
Perhaps one of your current customers is experiencing
those same problems, but instead of complaining he may
just stop buying and quietly tell his associates. Listen
to your best customers and to all the complainers—
they're telling you how to improve your business.

## McCAFFERTY'S LAW NUMBER TEN
**The only one who can really measure our performance is
the customer, and when he measures it, he's always right.**

One of my former bosses used to drive me crazy
telling me that the customer was always right. I knew
that wasn't true because we had so many who were
wrong: they ordered the wrong parts, they filled the
forms out incorrectly, and then they had the gall to
complain. He finally made me understand that the customer really *was* always right. When the customer ordered the wrong part, we should have explained to him

that there was a better one. When he filled out the order form incorrectly, we should have helped him correct it. Whenever anything happened that was not to the customer's liking, we were wrong in letting it happen, even if our error was in not communicating with the customer.

You can tell when customers are happy, because they buy services from you. Do the customers feel satisfied? Do they buy again? Do they tell others to buy from you? That's the ultimate measurement—business growth.

## MEASURING INDIVIDUAL PERFORMANCE

While we're on the subject of performance measurement, what about the performance of individuals? They need their performance measured, too, and there has to be a way to do it. We covered the evaluation of field managers in Chapter 7, but there are also the salespeople and the service people to consider.

Salespeople are relatively easy to evaluate. They either sold something or they didn't, and if they did you can count the number of items they sold or how many of each particular product. These are easy to measure, but are those numbers the entire measurement of a salesperson's effectiveness, and therefore of his value to the business?

How he relates to his territory can be another measurement. Since there are many customers in his territory, how many of them repeat? How many of them were using your contract preventive maintenance, but cancelled their contract with you? Was he aware of the problem before you told him you had a cancellation letter? Was he able to save the contract? When his customers are about to buy a service that you sell, do they automatically call him?

Then there is the evaluation of the service person. In some businesses such an evaluation may be simple, but in most it is not really done effectively because of the complexity of the problem. How, for example, can you measure the total effectiveness of a service person when he and the other service people in the office all work at various times for the same customers, and if you have specialized people, even on the same calls? The evaluation then becomes largely subjective, and all such measurements are subject to extreme error and even to bias. The error and bias are by the measurer; the frustration will be for the person being measured.

Despite its inherent imprecisions, there must be subjective measurement of things that cannot easily be quantified, and it will always be so. But with some thought, the situation can be improved, and we should strive to do so. Our people deserve the fairest and most accurate evaluation that we can give them. Just because something is difficult is no reason to say it can't be done. After all, if there were no problems, where would the service business be?

## DETERMINING PROFITABILITY

The first question to arise is whether or not you want to be a profit center, and after that, how profitable? The basic decision as to how profitable is based on how profitable you *want* it to be. The first approach of the manufacturing, sales, and marketing people will be to analyze the costs item by item and add a small markup so you can arrive at a "competitive" price.

This is based on their experience in bidding on all sales and on the fact that they are accustomed to cut the price in order to make the sale. It also has a base in the market share concept where a company such as yours is expected to have a certain percentage of the market.

### The market share concept

In the service business there is as yet no need for the market share concept, since no one has been able to calculate accurately the size of the total market. Since you are not after a specific share (like 40 percent), you are then after all you can get at the price you wish to charge for your services. If you maintain earthmovers, and a competitor charges $100 for a service, you can very easily charge $150 for the same service.

### McCAFFERTY'S LAW NUMBER ELEVEN
#### The selling price of your product is determined not by cost but by its value to the customer.

Therefore, it is not a matter of market share, but of performing a service valuable to the customer and charging what the customer thinks it is worth to him. Although this will normally allow you a high level of profit compared with new product sales, it is in no way a rip-off. Nothing is a rip-off when the customer thinks he is getting his money's worth, and is in reality getting a quality service. Its a matter of who takes the risk: if the customer performs his own service, he takes all the risk when he does not perform; when he hires you, he pays you to accept some or all of the risk of short equipment life and equipment failure. And if you plan to maintain your growth, when he pays you to accept risk, you'd better accept it. It also follows that there is no such thing as a free service. If at any time one of your costs escalates, you increase your prices and you don't cut your margin, so your profit remains protected.

This method of doing business is foreign to the sales and marketing group, and one of your greatest and continuing problems will be to convince them that you can do business this way. They will always have a feeling that you need to bid with all the competitors and "take your share." In reality, you should keep your prices up and skim off the customers who are willing to pay a premium for highly professional services.

### Other approaches to making profits

There are several other ways to approach the situation. A traditional way is to add up each cost as you go, put in some overhead and an amount of fixed profit, and arrive at a selling price. After the sale is made, you will have the opportunity to see whether you can afford to do the work for that amount of money, and any money left over is called profit. A problem with this approach is that as things happen along the way, the costs have a way of changing (almost always upward) and since the overhead and markup are limited and fixed, your amount of profit varies from day to day and from month to month.

There is another more dependable way to produce profit. First, you have to have an agreement with your sales organization that they will sell services for the prices you tell them to sell for. If the occasion demands, they are always allowed to charge more, but they are never allowed to reduce the selling price below the one that you have given them. And if they do, they will face severe disciplinary measures from you.

Once this is understood, you can develop the selling prices. These are based on your costs, of course, but with a slightly different touch: you base the price on your costs as well as you know them, and then you add whatever amount is necessary for the development of a minimum profit. This could be anywhere from 5% to 50%, depending on many factors. You now have the minimum selling price your salespeople are allowed to use. Now inform them of this, without explaining all the details. If they want to convince you that they really have a deep and abiding interest in the future of the company, they will of course add a bit of a markup when they sell services.

By nature, salespeople understand quite well that they could increase their sales if the prices were lower. Of course, they could, but then you wouldn't make the profit you want to. In these circumstances, it's your job to convince them that the prices are fair, even though they may be higher than the competition's, because you provide more and better services, so they're worth more. It's also your job to be certain at all times that your services *are* better.

## McCAFFERTY'S LAW NUMBER TWELVE
### Profit is a result of attitude, not of mathematics.

The most important remaining point is that as your costs increase or decrease, modify your pricing and keep a constant monitor on costs. This brings us back to reporting systems, which were first discussed in Chapter 5. Every time a cost is developed in common with another organization within the division (or company, or corporation), there is a tendency for the accountants to allocate the costs to the interested parties on the basis of some esoteric theory. For example, engineering cost within a division or group of divisions can be allocated to various departments on the basis of total sales volume, even though the sales of one department (service, in your case) may not involve much of the material engineered by the factory but will use a high percentage of material purchased elsewhere. It will seem logical to the accountants, and you may have no better idea for an allocation formula.

The point I'm trying to make is that the best possible way to run the business is to allocate nothing, but to charge each operating group with its real-life costs. You may run into a problem trying to decide how much of each corporate cost you really used, if any at all, and this is the area where you may have to give in on allocation. But when it comes to the costs within your division (like factory engineering and marketing, for example), don't give in—fight the complicated allocation and go for real costs. That way you can establish accurate pricing based on your business, and you can develop the amount of profit you feel is realistic in your industry.

Certain costs will always remain on allocation, and perhaps rightly so, since they are services available to all parts of the company, and each must pay its fair share. In cases like these, you will surely give in with a smile and tell them that you are delighted to carry your part of the load. It is still good policy, however, to complain from time to time (although in a reasonable manner) about the amount of the allocation, thereby ensuring more attention to the costs of the services allocated to you.

# 11

# Summary and conclusion

To me there are six words that should be the most important in the vocabulary of anyone who has the temerity to start a service business.

*Commitment.* Without this on the part of everyone involved, things just won't happen. For you, the driving force, it has to be a sense of mission. From your commitment will come that of others—your employees, your peers, your higher management. You have to *believe.*

*Creativity.* Anyone can start a business that performs the same way others do and that merely has a different name to identify it. To make your business really successful, it has to be better: it must do things better, offer better services, and hire and train better people. Change must not only be adapted to; it must be initiated. Creativity is not by any means limited to the arts. Better ways to paint trucks, improved reporting systems, more effective tools, better training programs, more effective motivational programs, better sales campaigns, an improved form for the stockroom clerk to use—they all require and are the direct result of creativity.

*Courage.* This is definitely not a requirement only for warriors. Although it's true that if your ideas are good enough and if you are a good enough salesperson you can always sell the ideas, it's not true that your ideas will always be sold in the time or in the manner that you had hoped for. If an idea of yours is premature or if there are higher priorities, it may take several years to make it real. You must have the courage to keep your fight alive. There will be times when you know that nobody else in the whole corporation understands the situation as you do, but you must have the courage to stand up for your opinion, when you think you are right. You must also have the courage to withstand those who have names for dreamers, creators, and innovators of the business world—names like nut, weirdo, maverick, and nonconformist.

*Practicality.* In any business environment it is very difficult to convert the theories and the creative ideas into practical methods and procedures that will work in the real world. The real difficulty is in deciding where the real world really is. No matter how well conceived, an idea will only be as good as how it works when it finally gets to the clerk or the service person who is expected to carry it out. Ideas that sound wonderful in the rarefied atmosphere of the home office may not work in the field, and it's up to you to change those ideas so that they *will* work.

*Humor.* Without a sense of humor, and a real sense of the ridiculous, who could survive all this?

*Flexibility.* This is where the adaptability to change and the acceptance of the ideas of others come in. To use a popular idiom, you have to stay loose. The world will change, and you will change. Accept that and use it as a tool rather than panicking when things don't go according to plan.

It's not enough to know the definitions of these six words; each of these concepts must be a part of your life. Business is a strange thing. You can go along for years, secure in the knowledge that you understand the basics of the whole thing, and all of a sudden it will hit you that reality is somewhat different from your conception of it. In simpler terms, you didn't understand the situation. There are some realities of business that you should be aware of, since that awareness may save you time and effort.

Although in training courses and business seminars there is great emphasis on the art and science of problem solving, you will find that the real results are obtained by exploiting opportunities rather than solving problems. An existing problem places a restriction on the capability of your business to get results, and the solution to the problem will merely eliminate the restriction and restore normality. Therefore, if you want to produce results, you must allocate your resources to opportunities rather than to problems. This would also suggest that effectiveness is more essential than efficiency.

It is also true that leadership, and only leadership, gets economic results; mere competence will not do the trick. Profit is the result obtained from making a unique or at least a distinct contribution. The contribution must be in a meaningful area, and the only ones who can decide whether what you do is meaningful are the marketplace and the customers. To paraphrase, the only way you can stay ahead of the competition is to be a leader—a leader in ideas, in technology, and in contributions to the industry of which you are a part. Positions of leadership are transitory, never permanent. If you are to stay out in front, you must work at it all the time. Your contributions today will become the normal operations of your competitors within a few years, and at that point you will have upgraded the industry. If you think that's not really the business you're in (teaching the competition to do better), you're not being realistic. This is where those six key words come in.

## McCAFFERTY'S LAW NUMBER THIRTEEN
### The only way to stay ahead of the competition is to be the acknowledged leader in your industry.

Remember that profits will be the result of the innovative advantage and will then disappear as soon as the innovation has become routine and someone else has seized the initiative. That's why to remain a leader you have to generate a constant flow of innovations. What exists today is already getting old, but many executives seem to spend most of their time working on the problems of yesterday, and more time trying to unmake the past than anything else.

## McCAFFERTY'S LAW NUMBER FOURTEEN
### It is always futile to restore "normality," which after all is only yesterday's reality.

So instead of going to all that effort to impose yesterday's norms on a present that is already different, the real objective is to change the business—its behavior, attitudes, expectations, directions, and measurements—as well as its products and markets.

What exists in the way of your resources is very likely to be misallocated. It's the old 80/20 rule: although 80 percent of the results are caused by 20 percent of the events, 80 percent of the costs are incurred by the remaining 80 percent of events, which have few results. In other words, costs and results are usually in an inverse relationship. Just for fun, change the word "costs" in the last sentences to "efforts": *efforts and results are in an inverse relationship!* Economic results are usually directly proportional to revenue, whereas your costs are directly proportional to the number of transactions such as service calls, purchases, and trips. The way it seems to work out is that if your resources and efforts are not monitored constantly, they will normally allocate themselves to the 80 percent of events that produce almost no results! When you think about it, this applies as much to what we do in our personal lives as it does in business. Its implications are really disturbing.

In order to create a business in a position of leadership, you have to be a leader. That requires many important qualities, including the six that have just been discussed and several others:

□ The ability to delegate authority is primary, especially in a new organization. As you build and develop your people, you must force yourself to let them do things *their* way. It is difficult to allow another person to do what you do well, and it's especially hard to do when you know that no one else could possibly do the job as well as you can. That attitude will remain until you really let someone else do it, and find out to your surprise that the task was accomplished more effectively than ever before. You have to develop your subordinate managers, because if you don't you'll be one of those managers who can never take two days for a meeting, can never be spared for a vacation, and always hauls that bulging briefcase home every night. That's not a very pleasant way to live. How can you lead if you have to be there managing every minute?

□ A true leader will pass all credits to his people and accept all blame himself.

□ The ability to gauge the risks involved in a course of action is most important. Although it is foolhardy to take a big risk for a small gain, it is equally foolhardy not to take a small risk that could result in a big gain. And somewhere along the line, you must understand that risks are not bad; they are an important part of life. They are not to be feared, but taken into account.

□ A real leader not only is creative himself, but provides a creative climate for his people. Subordinates must know that they have the freedom to try new ideas, which may fail, and not be punished for trying them. If this kind of supportive environment is not there, they will do their jobs in the routine and regulated manner that means eventual failure, since there will be no progress.

□ The true leader remains cool in the face of disaster. When the disaster is happening, he may go into a small private room and scream for a few moments, but to the world he will at all times present the appearance of composure. He always tries to keep in mind that most disasters can be converted into opportunities.

□ It is particularly true in these times that leaders must *really* be leaders. Our hands are tied in many ways by agencies, union rules, government edicts, and pressure groups. The real effect is a threat to creativity and imagination, and you must therefore work harder to keep from stifling them.

□ Leading and managing aren't the same thing. You manage by accomplishing, by having responsibility, by conducting operations. You lead by being out in front where it's never very crowded.

□ A leader must have the vision and strength to call the shots. It's a risky business, but if being a leader means that you must raise your head to see where you are about to lead, it also means that you'll be visible enough to shoot at and that once in a while you'll get hit.

Have you thought about what the future holds for your particular service business? How will you accomplish your goals ten years from now, assuming that you are at that time using the latest techniques? If you are servicing large units that can't be moved into a shop, your service people might be connecting the "customer" to your central computer through a phone coupler for trouble diagnosis. Perhaps you are already operating that way. Will you still have field service people? How will they operate, what tools will they use, and since such tools are probably not available now, where will you get them? If you wish to maintain leadership in your industry, you had better start designing the tools of the future. These are questions that must be asked, and must be answered if you are to lead. If you are content to follow, then your competitors will work out the answers for you.

> *There they go, and I must hurry, for*
> *I am their leader.*
> Anonymous

## CONCLUSION

After you have created your service business, started it off with the high profit and growth rates that are possible, and molded it in such a manner that it will run that way, something will happen. Your growth cycle—the period of creativity, innovation, entrepreneurship, of new and expanding markets—may take 10 to

20 years. The business will then be healthy and robust and can be maintained by other, perhaps less creative, people—the maintainers. Innovators are wonderful to have around when things need to be created and grown, but their constant presence sometimes makes others rather uncomfortable. You and your few key people, the innovators, will find yourselves in other positions, and the maintainers will take over the running of the business. Your only opportunity to remain in the same position of power at this time is probably to become a maintainer, and if you have truly been an innovator you won't be able to change, or won't even want to.

Since maintaining a business is like riding a bicycle (you either keep it moving or it falls over), there will be a slow and very gradual lessening of the drive to deliver the former high level of growth and profit, and the business will move from an industry position of leadership. This, too, will happen over a period of years, and the change each year will be almost unnoticeable. Then there will appear upon the scene a young and eager innovator, who will somehow attain a position of enough responsibility to affect the direction of the business, and the whole cycle will start over.

In my experience, already established organizations are highly resistant to change, and new organizations very rapidly become established ones. As the creators and managers of the service industry, we have the responsibility to build our businesses and our people in such a manner that we at once become aware of a change and are able to use it to our advantage almost immediately. The service business is a worthwhile endeavor. Its very name shows it to be a service to the people who are our customers. By helping them to prosper, we will prosper, too.

# McCAFFERTY'S LAWS

1. No one understands your business as well as you do. You will spend the rest of your life explaining it to others.

2. The service you are offering your customers must be made available to them in their location.

3. The successful service business will be the one that delivers to its customers the services they need and want.

4. Should customers not fully understand their needs and wants, it is your responsibility to explain them.

5. The only real source of money is customers.

6. Before you ever agree to put anything on a computer, make sure it works!

7. It's better to try something and fail, than to do nothing and succeed.

8. Always hire people smarter than yourself.

9. The services you provide must be performed in a highly professional manner.

10. The only one who can really measure our performance is the customer, and when he measures it, he's always right.

11. The selling price of your product is determined not by cost but by its value to the customer.

12. Profit is a result of attitude, not of mathematics.

13. The only way to stay ahead of the competition is to be the acknowledged leader in your industry.

14. It is always futile to restore "normality," which after all is only yesterday's reality.

# Index